Jorge Gómez
Velssy Hernández
Daniel Salas

DESIGN AND IMPLEMENTATION OF ONTOLOGIES IN JAVA AND APACHE JENA

Jorge Gómez
Velssy Hernández
Daniel Salas

DESIGN AND IMPLEMENTATION OF ONTOLOGIES IN JAVA AND APACHE JENA

Ontology building and deployment in Java

ScienciaScripts

Imprint

Any brand names and product names mentioned in this book are subject to trademark, brand or patent protection and are trademarks or registered trademarks of their respective holders. The use of brand names, product names, common names, trade names, product descriptions etc. even without a particular marking in this work is in no way to be construed to mean that such names may be regarded as unrestricted in respect of trademark and brand protection legislation and could thus be used by anyone.

Cover image: www.ingimage.com

This book is a translation from the original published under ISBN 978-620-3-03102-7.

Publisher:
Sciencia Scripts
is a trademark of
International Book Market Service Ltd., member of OmniScriptum Publishing Group
17 Meldrum Street, Beau Bassin 71504, Mauritius
Printed at: see last page
ISBN: 978-620-3-40240-7

ABOUT THE AUTHORS:

Jorge Gómez Gómez

Systems Engineer, received a Master's degree in Telematics Engineering at the University of Cauca Colombia in 2010, PhD in Information Technology and Communications at the University of Granada Spain in 2018, Full-time professor of the Systems Engineering program - University of Cordoba, Member IEEE Branch. Research interests: Ubiquitous Computing and Advanced Services in Telecommunications. Researcher in the SOCRATES research group - University of Cordoba.

Velssy Hernández Riaño

She is a Systems Engineer and holds a Master's degree in Telematics Engineering from the Universidad Francisco José de Caldas, Colombia. She is a Professor and Researcher in the SOCRATES research group of the Department of Systems Engineering at the University of Córdoba.

Daniel Salas Álvarez

Systems Engineer and Master in Computer Science, with 22 years of experience in University Teaching, as a researcher I have published 3 books, more than 20 scientific publications, with experience in the development and coordination of projects for the incorporation of Information and Communication Technologies in basic education and higher education. I have served as Dean of the Faculty of Engineering at the University of Cordoba, for five years, 10 years as director of the Research Group SOCRATES, Editor of the Journal Engineering and Innovation for 3 years, Academic Vice Chancellor (e), Rector (e) on several occasions, I have participated in committees of experts in the Ministry of National Education, 12 years of experience as an academic peer at the Ministry of National Education, Academic Peer to the CNA and four (4) years of experience as Academic Peer in Colciencias. Currently I am a member of the IEEE with Membership No 95671027, member of the Inclusive Learning Initiative Network and the World Network of Researchers, AuthorAID, Founding Member of the International Cava Congress.

SUMMARY

The use of ontologies for data representation is a wide-ranging line of research in artificial intelligence. Ontologies aim to represent knowledge so that it can be interpreted by computer systems. The applications of ontologies are varied, ranging from data representation to the semantic web, expert systems and others. This book initially explains the most common methodologies for the development of ontologies, ranging from the simple methodology, through the Skeletal, to the NeON, each one has its own characteristics that make it useful depending on the problem to be modelled and the adoption of the knowledge engineer. Next, a semantic representation model is proposed to describe a university environment, and then an ontology is built in Protegé. Finally, Java and Apache Jena are used to execute desktop queries and web services.

The reader will have an immersive experience in the development of ontologies, so that even if they do not know much about the subject, once they start with the theoretical foundation and aspects related to the properties of ontologies, they will be able to develop an ontology step by step from scratch. It is important to highlight that the management of ontologies has a great field of action in the world of artificial intelligence, therefore we recommend that readers, when they finish reading and executing the guides in this book, continue to consolidate this knowledge in problems of greater complexity and apply them in real environments.

Content

CHAPTER I: THEORETICAL UNDERPINNINGS

1. Methodologies for Ontology Development

The ontology design process requires a methodology for its development. This section briefly describes the existing methodologies in the literature. As can be seen in the methodologies, most of the ontologies have the same phases and the activities are repeated. Figure 1 presents the generic life cycle for the development of ontologies.

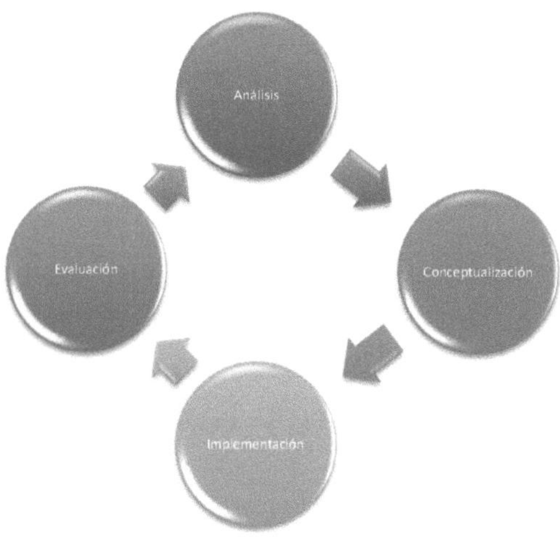

Figure 1 Ontology development lifecycle

The general process for the development of an ontology, which consists of four phases, is briefly explained below:
- Analysis Phase: This phase contemplates the purpose of the ontology that will allow defining the scope, domain, and reusability of the ontology.
- Conceptualisation Phase: In this stage a conceptual model describing the ontology to be developed is defined, where it must comply with the specification obtained in the previous phase. Conceptualisation consists of organising and converting an informal perception of a domain into a semi-formal specification, using intermediate representations such as diagrams or tables, which can be understood by domain experts and ontology developers. Different methodologies propose the use of different conceptual models, from incomplete informal models such as the mind

maps used in (Sure et al., 2002) to semi-formal models such as the binary relationship diagram or the concept dictionary proposed in (Fernandez et al., 1999).

- Implementation: This refers to the explicit representation of the knowledge acquired in the previous phase in a formal language. That is, it involves the generation of computational models according to the syntax of a formal representation language such as RDF(S), OWL and FLogic, among others.
- Evaluation: Consists of making a technical judgement of the ontology, its associated software environment and documentation against a framework during each phase and between phases of its life cycle (Gomez et al., 1995). The reference framework may include requirements specifications, competency questions and/or the real world.

There are many existing methodologies, in this paper we only briefly describe some of the methodologies, starting with the simple knowledge engineering methodology, SKELETAL, METHONTOLOGY, **On-To-Knowledge,** DILIGENT and ending with the NEON Methodology.

1.1. Simple Knowledge Engineering Methodology (Noy and MacGuinness, 2001)

Step 1. Determine the scope and domain of the ontology. Ontology development is initiated by defining the domain and scope of the ontology. Competency questions (Gruninger and Fox 1995) can be used to determine the domain and scope of the ontology by defining a set of questions that the ontology should be able to answer, through its knowledge base.

Step 2. Consider reusing existing ontologies. It is important to check existing sources for the domain of interest. Especially, if the system to be developed needs interaction with other applications that involve particular ontologies or vocabularies.

Step 3. Specify important terms in the ontology. Making a complete list of terms makes it easier to identify the concepts to be represented, as well as their properties and relationships between them.

Step 4. Define classes and class hierarchy. From various approaches to develop class hierarchies, the most general and domain-specific concepts can be defined (Uschold and Gruninger 1996), such as the processes of *top-down*, *bottom-up* and the process that combines the two, among others.

Step 5. Define the properties of the slot classes. The classes alone do not provide enough information to answer the questions in step 1. Once some of the classes have been defined, the internal structure of the concepts has to be described. Then select the classes from the list of terms, which has been created in step 3. Most of the remaining terms are likely to be properties of these classes. For each property in the list, you have to determine which class it describes. In general, there are several types of object properties that can become slots in an ontology: i) intrinsic properties, ii) extrinsic properties, iii) relations to other individuals; these are the relations between the individual members of the class and other elements.

Step 6. Define the facets of the slots. Slots can have different facets that describe the type of value, the allowed values, the number of values (cardinality), and other characteristics of the slot values they can take. The most common are: a) Slot cardinality, which defines how many slots can have. Some systems distinguish only between single cardinality, allowing at most one value, and multiple cardinality allowing any number of values. b) Value type describes what types of values can fill the slot, e.g. string, numeric, instance type and enumerated. c) Domain and range of a slot, the classes allowed for slots of type Instance are often called a range of a slot. The classes to which a slot is attached, or to a class describing the property of a slot, are called the domain of the slot.

Step 7. Create instances. The last step is the creation of individual instances of classes in the hierarchy. Defining an individual instance of a class requires, choosing a class, creating an individual instance of that class and filling in the values of the slot.

1.2. SKELETAL METHODOLOGY

This methodology defines a set of steps that are required for the understanding and construction of the ontology (Uschold and King, 1995). In order to identify and define the key concepts of concepts and relationships based on natural language terms. Skeletal proposes the following four steps:

Step 1. Identify the purpose of the ontology. It is necessary to identify why the ontology is being built and its possible uses, as well as the range of users of the ontology. Competency questions allow you to identify the purpose of the ontology in specific terms.

Step 2. Ontology building. Building the ontology requires three steps: capturing, encoding and integrating existing ontologies.

Ontological capture refers to:

1. Identification of the key concepts and relationships in the domain.

2. Production of precise and unambiguous definitions for such concepts and relationships.

3. Identification of terms to refer to such concepts and relationships.

Coding consists of explicitly representing the conceptualisation captured in the previous stage in a formal language. This involves the choice of a meta-ontology, a representation language and the generation of the code.

The integration of existing ontologies is a key point in developing an ontology that can be shared among multiple user communities. However, it is a complex problem as it requires explicit agreement on all the assumptions underlying the ontologies to be integrated.

Step 3. Evaluation. A technical judgement of the ontologies, associated software environment and documentation should be made against requirements specifications, competency questions and the real world.

Step 4. Documentation. Suggests documenting the main concepts defined in the ontology and the primitives used to express the definitions in the ontology, also called metaontology.

1.3. METHONTOLOGY

Methontology allows the construction of ontologies by identifying the activities required in the ontology development process, the life cycle based on evolutionary prototypes and particular techniques to perform, use and evaluate the activities generated in the development process (Gómez-Pérez et al., 2003).

In the ontology development process, activities can be classified into three categories Figure 2: a) management activities, b) development-oriented activities and c) support activities.

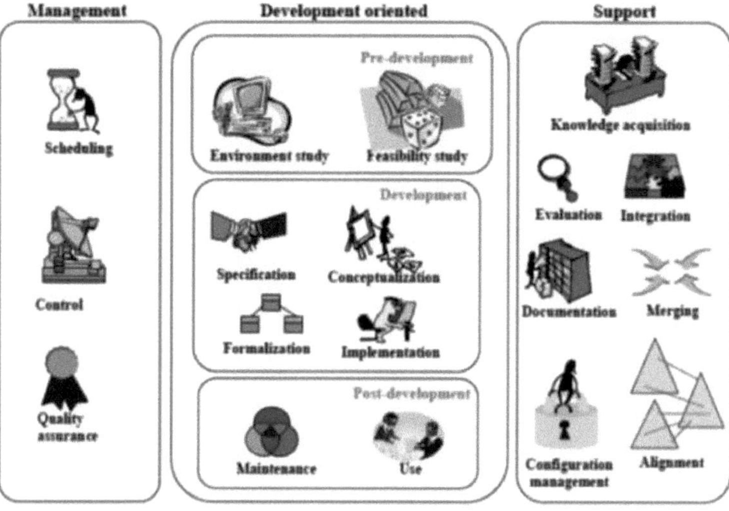

Figure 2. Process for ontology development (Gómez-Pérez et al., 2003).

The ontology development process does not identify the order in which activities are to be performed. Therefore, the lifecycle determines when the activities should be carried out. That is, it identifies the set of stages through which the ontology moves during its lifetime; describing which activities are to be performed at each stage and how these stages are related.

1.4. On-To-Knowledge Methodology (Staab et al., 2001)

The On-To-Knowledge methodology (Staab et al., 2001) allows the construction of knowledge management oriented ontologies. The development processes of the methodology are: feasibility study, initiation, refinement, evaluation and maintenance Figure 3.

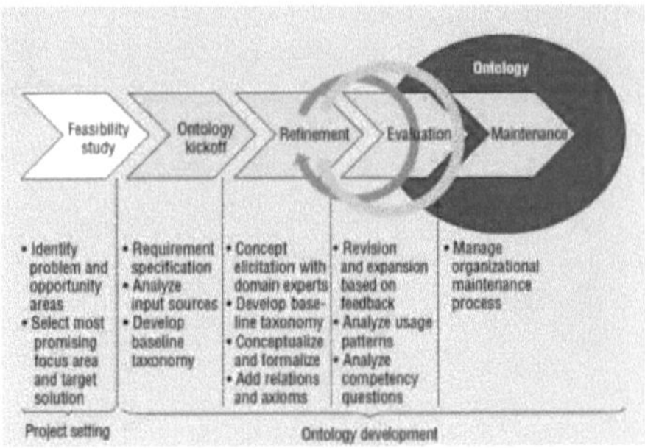

Figure 3. On-To-Knowledge ontology development process. Adapted from (Stabb, 2001).

A feasibility study should be conducted to identify problem or opportunity areas and possible solutions. The feasibility study can help determine the economic and technical viability of the project, and should be carried out before developing the ontology because it serves as a basis for the start-up phase.

Ontology initiation should generate an ontology requirements specification document. It should also guide an ontology engineer in decisions about inclusion, exclusion and hierarchical structure of concepts in the ontology. At this initial stage, it is necessary to look for already developed and potentially reusable ontologies.

In the refinement phase, a mature, application-oriented target ontology is obtained according to the specification generated in the previous phase. It is divided into different sub-phases:

- Compilation of an informal reference taxonomy containing the relevant concepts given during the initiation phase.
- Obtain domain expert knowledge based on the initial input from the reference taxonomy, to develop a seed ontology containing relevant concepts and describing the relationships between them.
- Transfer from seed ontology to target ontology using formal representation languages.

The evaluation phase allows verifying whether the target ontology satisfies the ontology requirements specification document and whether the ontology supports or answers the competence questions analysed in the project initiation phase. Reaching the level specified in the target ontology may require several cycles of evaluation and refinement.

Finally, the maintenance phase updates changes to the ontology specifications, through the development of new versions, and tests the ontology in the target application environment.

1.5. DILIGENT METHODOLOGY

Diligent (Pinto et al., 2004) is a methodology for the development of ontologies in a distributed manner, supporting domain experts who can work collaboratively and geographically dispersed. The development process includes five main activities: (1) construction, (2) local adaptation, (3) analysis, (4) revision, (5) local update.

The construction activity is performed taking into account domain experts, users, knowledge engineers and ontology engineers, who draft an initial ontology Figure 4. Once the ontology is available, users can adapt it locally for their particular purposes. In the analysis stage, similarities in user ontologies are identified, and the different needs of users are taken into account to satisfy their evolving requirements, and the roles and functions of the methodology are shown in Figure 4.

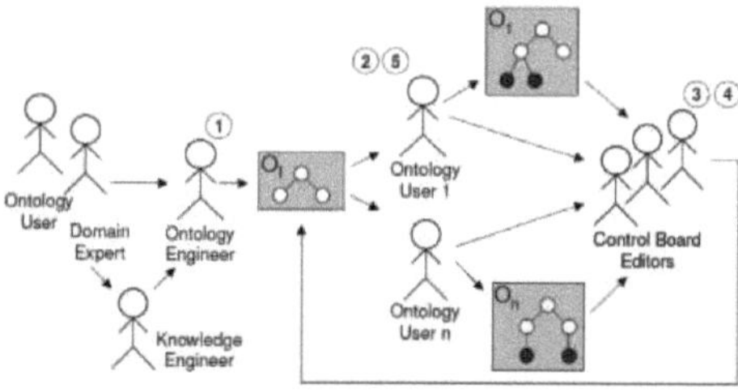

Figure 4. Roles and functions of Diligent. Adapted from (Pinto et al., 2004)

The *board* should regularly review the shared ontology, so that the local ontologies do not stray too far from the shared ontology. Therefore, the board should have a balanced and representative participation of the different types of participants involved in the process. Once a new version of the shared ontology is available, users can update their own local ontologies to better use the knowledge represented in the new version. Users can reuse the new concepts represented in the new version, instead of using their corresponding previously locally defined concepts.

1.6. NEON METHODOLOGY

The NeOn methodology uses as a solution strategy the decomposition of a general problem into different subproblems to be solved (Suárez, 2010). This methodology allows the construction of ontological networks based on scenarios, which are composed of processes and activities. To obtain the solution to the general problem, i.e. the development of an ontological network, solutions to the different subproblems, represented in nine scenarios in figure 5, must be combined.

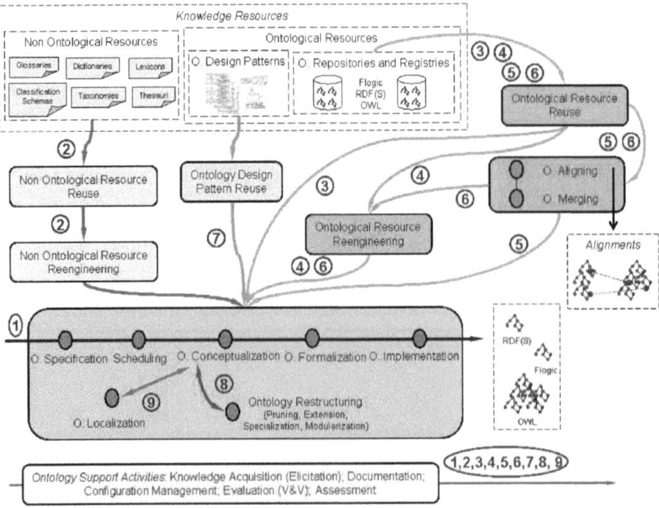

Figure 5. Scenarios for building ontologies and ontology networks. (Suarez, 2010)

The nine most common scenarios that can occur during the development of the ontology network are the following:

Scenario 1: from specification to implementation. The ontology network is developed from scratch, i.e. without reusing available knowledge resources.

Scenario 2: reuse and re-engineering of non-ontology resources. Ontology developers should carry out the non-ontology resource reuse process to decide, according to the requirements of the ORSD (ontology requirements specification document), which NORs (non-ontology resource reuse) can be reused to build the ontology network. The selected NORs should then be redesigned into ontologies.

Scenario 3: Reuse of ontology resources. Ontology developers use ontology resources (ontologies in general, ontology modules and/or ontology declarations).

Scenario 4: reuse and re-engineering of ontology resources. Ontology developers reuse and re-engineer ontology resources.

Scenario 5: reuse and merging of ontology resources. This scenario is developed only in cases where several ontology resources in the same domain are selected for reuse and when ontology developers wish to create a new ontology resource from two or more ontology resources.

Scenario 6: reuse, merge and re-engineer ontology resources. Ontology developers reuse, merge and re-engineer ontology resources in the construction of ontology networks. This scenario is similar to Scenario 5; however, here developers decide not to use the combined set of resources as is, but to redesign it.

Scenario 7: reuse of ontology design patterns (ODP). Ontology developers access ODP repositories for reuse.

Scenario 8: Restructuring of ontology resources. Ontology developers restructure (modularisation, pruning, extension and/or specialisation) ontology resources to integrate them into the ontology network being built.

Scenario 9: Localisation of ontology resources. Ontology developers adapt an ontology to other languages and cultural communities, resulting in a multilingual ontology.

CHAPTER II: MODELLING FOR A LEARNING SCENARIO

When modelling the context, it is important to take into account some characteristics of contextual information, as outlined by (Henricksen et al, 2002):

- Context information shows a range of temporal characteristics, these can be static or dynamic. In the case of static information, the information will always be invariant, e.g. a person's date of birth. Normally context information is changeable, which implies the use of dynamic characteristics, such as the location of a learner, the learning activities to be performed at a given time, among others.
- Imperfect context information. Information may be incorrect if the modelling does not reflect the true state of the world, inconsistent if it contains contradictory information, or incomplete if some aspects of the context are not known. Therefore, it is important to consider all aspects related to the context, in order to prevent them from leading to bad modelling.
- The context has many representation alternatives. The context model must support multiple representations of the same context, in different forms and at different levels of abstraction, and must be available to capture the relationship that exists between representation alternatives.
- Context information is highly interrelated. Context information can be related by derivations of rules, which describe how information is obtained by one or more pieces of information.

As a result of the initial literature review on learning systems that respond to the interaction needs of the learner and the system, ontology-based modelling is adopted as the most appropriate technique for context management. Ontologies enable knowledge exchange by providing a formal specification of the semantics of the data. They allow heterogeneous and distributed entities in mobile and ubiquitous environments to exchange information (Bettini et al., 2010). Ontological approaches based on the use of the OWL language enhance the support of automated reasoning by enabling the representation of complex data; providing a formal semantics for context data that allows sharing and/or integrating context between different sources; providing reasoning tools to check the consistency of a set of relations describing a contextual situation and finally, most importantly, the characterisation of a more abstract context from the recognition of a set of contextual data and their interrelationships, e.g. recognising user activity automatically (Perera et al, 2014; Bettini et al, 2010).

The purpose of the development of this ontology is to generate a semantic model that represents all the elements found in a learning environment, in such a way that it can be interpreted and processed. In order to respond to the educational needs of the students under the principles of active learning, in such a way that it allows to generate interaction between the students and the context.

2. Ontology components

Individuals represent objects in the domain of interest and are also known as instances.

2.1. Properties in OWL

Properties are binary relations on individuals and can be inverse, transitive or   symmetric.

2.2. Classes at OWL

OWL classes are understood as sets that contain individuals and can be organised within a hierarchy of classes and subclasses known as a taxonomy. Classes are also known as concepts, as they are a concrete representation of concepts.

2.3. Descriptive Logic and OWL

First-order logic

The foundation that guarantees the logical purity of ontologies is first-order logic. Descriptive logics (DL) as well as OWL are based on it.

Why we use descriptive logics: First-order logic is undecidable (it is easy to assert things about objects, but computationally complex) Formal language is required to construct and combine category definitions (e.g. subset and superset relations) Semantic reasoners are based on it: FACT++, Rancer, Pellet, ...

2.4. Descriptive logic

Knowledge representation languages

DL was designed as an extension of semantic frameworks and networks, equipped with logic-based semantics.

Characteristics :

A descriptive formalism: concepts, roles (relationships), individuals.

A terminological formalism: axioms describing generic properties.

An assertive formalism: it introduces properties of individuals.

2.5. Descriptive logic

Main inference tasks with descriptive logic:

Subsumption (checking whether one category is a subset of another)

Classification (checking whether an object belongs to a category)

Example: Single= Y(NotMarried, Adult, Adult, Male) Single(x)=> NotMarried(x)YAdult(x)YMale(x) (first order logic)

Example: performs automatic classification (performed by the language-reasoner's inference engine) at runtime.

2.6. Correspondence between OWL and DL

DL Architecture

Descriptive logics : TBOX

Tbox: contains general terminology statements. Vocabulary of an application domain according to: Concepts, Roles, etc. They are of two types.

Descriptive logics : TBOX

Abox: contains assertions (instances) about concrete elements and relations of the domain. That is, they are assertions about individuals using vocabulary. Two types:

Formalise in DL and then in OWL DL

Definition of concepts.

Grass and trees are plants. Leaves are part of the tree, but there are other parts of a tree that are not leaves. A dog should at least eat bones. A sheep is an animal that should only eat grass. A giraffe is an animal that should only eat leaves. Mad cows only eat brains that belong to sheep.

Restrictions:

Animals are disjunct with plants.

Properties:

Eat is applied to animals and its inverse is eaten_by.

Individuals Tom Flossie is a cow Rex is a dog and is a pet of Mick Fido is a dog Tibbs is a cat

2.7. Relationships and entities

Entities, also called concepts, represent the elements of the context. The concept represents a group of different individuals, which share common characteristics; they can be more or less specific. The class has a number of properties that allow it to be defined. In figure 1, the convention of representation is shown. For the purpose of this ontology the main classes are:

- Student
- Professor
- Device
- Activity
- Learning object
- Weather
- Location
- Planning
- Event
- Role

Relationships describe the interactions between concepts or properties of an entity.

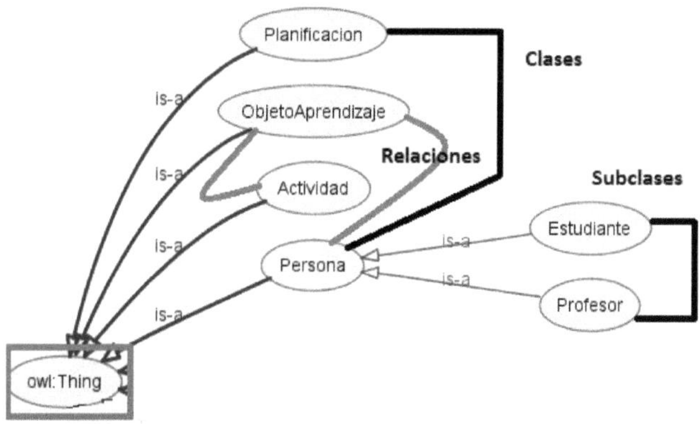

Figure 1. Schematic representation of an ontology

2.8. Applied methodology for ontology development

For the purposes of the development of this doctoral thesis, the NeoN methodology has been taken as a reference, because it proposes the use of ontological networks, which facilitates the creation of new ontologies from existing ones. It also proposes a methodological guide that allows working in detail on processes and activities related to the creation and reuse of ontologies. In this doctoral thesis the NeOn methodology is adopted, because it allows the reuse of existing ontologies, to adjust it to the ontological network model of the contextual awareness system proposed in this work.

By adopting the NeOn methodology, some of the scenarios proposed for the development of the ontology are taken. In the first instance, scenario 1 will be addressed, followed by scenario 3 and scenario 5.

- **Development of ontology networks from specification to implementation**. As the purpose of this work is to develop an ontology that allows the student to interact with their environment under the concept of contextual awareness and that in turn the environment facilitates learning activities. To achieve this purpose, the NeOn methodology requires in the first instance that scenario 1 is mandatory for the development of the ontology, this will allow to define which elements to integrate into the ontological network. The ontologies selected to build the ontological network that will describe the knowledge base of the system are then defined, given the problems posed. Figure 2 shows the ontological network.

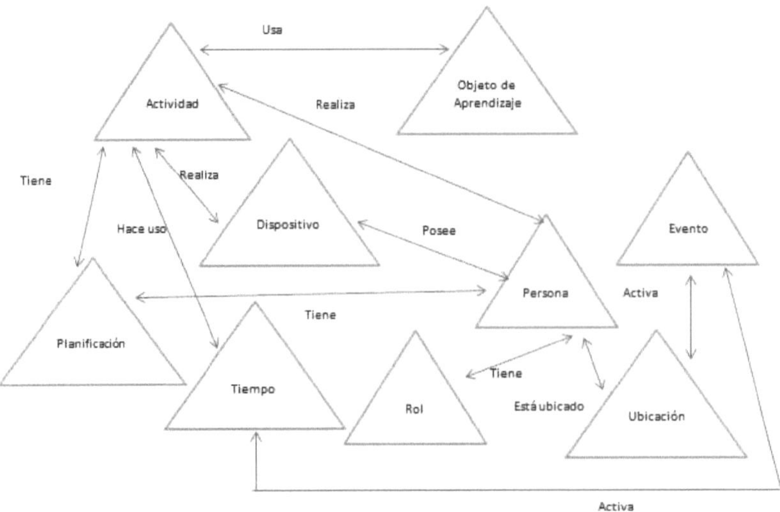

Figure 2 Ontological network for a context-aware system

The ontological network for a context-aware system that allows the learner to interact with the context is briefly described below: people are located in a Location, the person has a role, for example four people are in the classroom, where each of these people are developing a different role, person 1, person 2, person 3 are students and person 4 is the tutor, therefore according to the situation the person executes a certain role, person performs an activity, for example person 1, person 2, person 3 are doing activity 1, person 4 is doing activity 2, the activity makes use of learning object, activity 1 makes use of learning object1, the activity makes use of time, activity 1 lasts 1 hour, a person has a device that allows him/her to perform learning activities. A learning activity has a schedule that has to be completed in a certain time. A learning activity can use 1 or more learning objects. An event can be triggered in a certain period of time, a location, an action performed by a person, which can lead to a notification to perform a learning activity.

2.9. Proposed ontology

This model will allow structuring the set of relationships and entities involved for an intelligent learning environment. This will allow the generation of an understandable vocabulary for the whole system. This will allow contextual information to provide the context-aware system with adaptive functionalities based on the situations that arise in an educational environment, the specifications are shown in table 1.

Table 1: Ontology requirements specification (Suárez-Figueroa, 2010)

1	Purpose
	The purpose of ontology construction is to model the learner's context in an intelligent environment. To enable learners to access learning resources, whereby information is tailored to the needs of each learner based on contextual data.
	Outreach
	The ontological network makes it possible to generate the knowledge base that makes it possible to respond to the interaction needs of the learner and his or her learning environment. For this purpose, the ontological network includes the subdomains of: location, time, device, learning objects, person, activity, environment, role and environments.
	Implementation language
	To be implemented in OWL and SWRL and developed in Protege 5.0.
	Intended end uses
	Students and teachers
5	Intended uses
	Ontology is used to define the contextual information of an intelligent learning environment. This will provide contextual awareness to the environment, allowing the learner's experience to be enriched by providing information that is generated from interaction with the context. The following is a list of some of the uses: - Addition, modification and deletion of student profile and role related

		information
		- Addition, modification and deletion of information related to the person's role
		- Adding, modifying and deleting information related to device information
		- Adding, modifying and deleting information related to learning objects
		- Adding, modifying and deleting information related to the learning activities to be undertaken by the learners
		- Adding, modifying and deleting information related to student work schedules
		- Addition, modification and deletion of information related to learning environments, this refers to the physical environments where the student will perform learning activities (classrooms, library, laboratories, auditoriums, outdoors, among others).
		- Localisation of learning objects, learners and locations
		-
	Ontology requirements	
6.1.	Non-functional requirements	
	The ontological model builds on widely recognised existing models	
6.2.	Functional requirements	

	R1. What are the access times to the physical and virtual environments for students? In the physical environments from Monday to Friday from 07:00 hours and 00 minutes until 21:00 hours and 00 minutes.
	R2. What are the locations where the lecturers will teach? Pre-assigned engineering building classrooms and laboratories.
	R3. What are the timetables assigned for teachers to teach the courses? Monday to Friday from 07:00 hours to 21:00 hours, depending on the course assignment.
	R4. At what time, date and place is the student Jorge assigned to develop the learning activity on electrical circuits? The student Jorge must attend on 14 July 2017 at 16:00 in room 204 of the Bioclimatic building of the Faculty of Engineering.
	R5. What activity has the student Jorge assigned on 14 July 2017 at 16:00 and what learning objects will he receive? The student Jorge will have a workshop on the subject of electromagnetism and the learning objects he will receive are electric field, magnetic field and electric charges.
	R5. What is the time interval in which student Jorge will carry out the learning activity on parallel circuits? The time interval that the student will have to carry out the learning activity will be on 14 July 2017 from 16:00 to 18:00 on the same day.
	R6. What device will the teacher be able to use to conduct his or her class?
	  - Personal computer
	  - Smartphone
	  - Laboratory tablets
	  - Board or blackboard
	  - Projector
	  - Wifi network
	R7. Who are the people who are close to the Electricity lab? engineering student	

	and teachers
	R8. What device will the learner have to carry out the learning activity?
	   - Personal computer
	   - Smartphone
	   - Laboratory tablets
	   - NFC tags
	   - QRCODE tags
	   - BLE sensors
	   - Laboratory Wifi network
	   - Bluetooth on smartphones and tablets
	R9. What learning activities are there to do today in the Introduction to Electrical Engineering course? Study of series circuits
	R10. What state should smartphones be in when they arrive in the classroom? They must have wifi enabled, bluetooth enabled, NFC enabled.
	R11. Which learning objects should be sent to introductory electrical engineering students before they go to class, learning objects on electrical conductors?
	R12. What events associated with the topics covered in class are planned for today, where? Workshop on Ohm's law, in the faculty's electricity laboratory at 18:00.
	R13. What event is currently taking place near the place of instruction that is related to the topic under discussion? Conference on gravitational fields, Faculty auditorium.
	R14 How to monitor the teaching and learning process of students? The monitoring of the teaching and learning process of students can be done inside and outside the classroom (laboratory, library, auditoriums).
	
	R15. If the student has a laptop and is at the university on day X at time h, can he see the following subjects? He/she will be able to see according to the course plan the subjects assigned for that day.

7.	Pre-glossary of terms
a)	Terms of competence questions and general characteristics

	- Environments
	   - Physicist
	   - Virtual
	   - Students
	   - Learning objects
	   - Weather
	   - Interval
	   - Device
	   - Learning activities
	   - Day
	   - Place
	   - State
	   - Laboratory
	   - Event
	   - Planning

		- Moment
		- Teachers
b)	Terms of responses	
		- Physical environment
		- Days of the week
		- Hours
		- Minutes
		- Classrooms
		- Buildings
		- Laboratories
		- Attend
		- Student
		- To be held
		- Workshop
		- Learning objects
		- Time interval
		- Learning activity
		- Personal computer
		- Smartphone
		- Laboratory tablets
		- Board or blackboard
		- Projector
		- Wifi network
		- NFC tags
		- QRCODE tags
		- BLE sensors
		- Auditorium
C)	Objects	
		- Personal computer
		- Smartphone
		- Laboratory tablets
		- NFC tags
		- QRCODE tags
		- BLE sensors
		- Wifi network
		- Laboratory
		- Monday to Friday
		- From 07:00 to 21:00
		- Faculty of Engineering
		- Faculty Auditorium
		- Laboratories

2.9.1. Re-use of ontological resources

The use of ontology to model context has been widely used as in (Chen et al, 2003: Chen et al, 2004; Wang 2004; Strang et al, 2004; Klyne et al, 2004; Pung et al, 2004; Bettini et al, 2010; Xu et al, 2013; Perera et al, 2014). However, despite its extensive study, there is no standard ontology that can solve problems such as the one posed in this thesis. The vast majority of ontologies obey particular application solutions, so that one way to define a context model is to take advantage of the solutions already proposed and reuse them. According to (Suarez-Figueroa, 2010), one way to take advantage of the work already done is through the development of ontological networks by reusing ontological resources.

In this scenario, the aim is to analyse existing ontologies in order to build the ontology network to be developed. This helps to a large extent to speed up the process of building the ontology network. To this end, it should be borne in mind that there are two types of ontologies, general and domain-specific. On the other hand, there are specific knowledge ontologies, which provide a knowledge base on different types of applications such as education, health, e-commerce, among others.

2.9.2. Re-use of general or common ontologies

General or common ontologies (Van et al, 1997; Mizoguchi et al, 1995; Xiang et al, 2010; Jimeno-Yepes et al 2009) pose general concepts based on theoretical foundations, which represent a knowledge base of different domains, such as spatio-temporal ontologies and mereology (Shoham, 1987; Bochman, 1990; Freundschuh and Egenhofer, 1997; Ye et al, 2007).

The general ontologies of time modelling, integrated in the ontological network of the contextual awareness system, are described below.

- **Time modelling**. Corresponds to concepts related to temporal aspects, such as hour, minute, second, millisecond, nanosecond, or date (day, month, year), in particular. Time modelling is used to control the set of actions that are executed at a given time. Numerous works address the concept of time as in (Shoham, 1987; Bochman, 1990; Freundschuh and Egenhofer, 1997; Ye et al, 2007), where they conceive it as an interval and a unit. They further classify it into calendar time or clock time. For example, by way of context a day is considered a point in time, in another scenario, it can be an interval of time. In this paper an analysis is made of the different ontologies developed to model time.

According to (Fernández-López and Gómez-Pérez, 2004), table 2 shows some features that implement time theories and that are necessary for the development of the context ontology for this work.

Table 2, Notions of weather modelling adapted from (Fernández-López and Gómez-Pérez, 2004).

Notions		Description
Time points	Appropriate intervals	You can see time points as in the timeline.
Time intervals	Temporary granularities	A time interval can be viewed as the time between two time points.
Absolute and relative time	Total order	Time is represented in an absolute way when it is related to one fact and is relative when it is related to the valid time of another fact.
Relationships between time intervals	infinite	It presents the relationship between time intervals, for example: is within (interval1, interval2), is before (Interval1, interval2), is equal to (interval1, interval2), starts at (interval1, interval2), ends at (interval1, interval2). (Allen, 1984)
Convex and non-convex intervals	Density	Non-convex intervals allow the identification of periodic intervals with gaps between them (e.g., "every Monday"). Convex intervals are those that are not composed of separate pieces (e.g., 30 January 2016l) (Zhou et al., 2000).
Open and closed intervals	Isomorphism to the real numbers	The end points of the interval may or may not be included in the interval.

Based on the notions put forward by (Fernández-López and Gómez-Pérez, 2004), the following general time use ontologies were analysed to model the temporal context. These ontologies were analysed because they conform to the OWL format and it is the implementation language for the ontology network. Table 3 describes the characteristics of the different ontologies that implement theories of time.

Table 3. Description of ontologies that implement theories of time. Adapted from (Fernández-López and Gómez-Pérez, 2004).

Features	OWL-Time	Sumo	AK-Time	Required for the network ontology of the contextual awareness system
Time points	Yes	Yes	Yes	Yes
Time intervals	Yes	Yes	Yes	Yes
Relationships	Yes	Yes	Yes	Yes
Time zones	Yes	Yes	No	Yes

Following the NeOn methodology and analysing the four dimensions (reuse costs, comprehension effort, integration effort and reliability) in the ontologies presented. The ontology that best suits the requirements of the ontological network of the contextual awareness system is OWL-Time.

For the purposes of the ontology model of the contextual awareness system, the ontology representing the time domain is created, in which the process of importing the general OWL-Time ontology is carried out. Figure 3 shows the integration of the ontology into the ontology network.

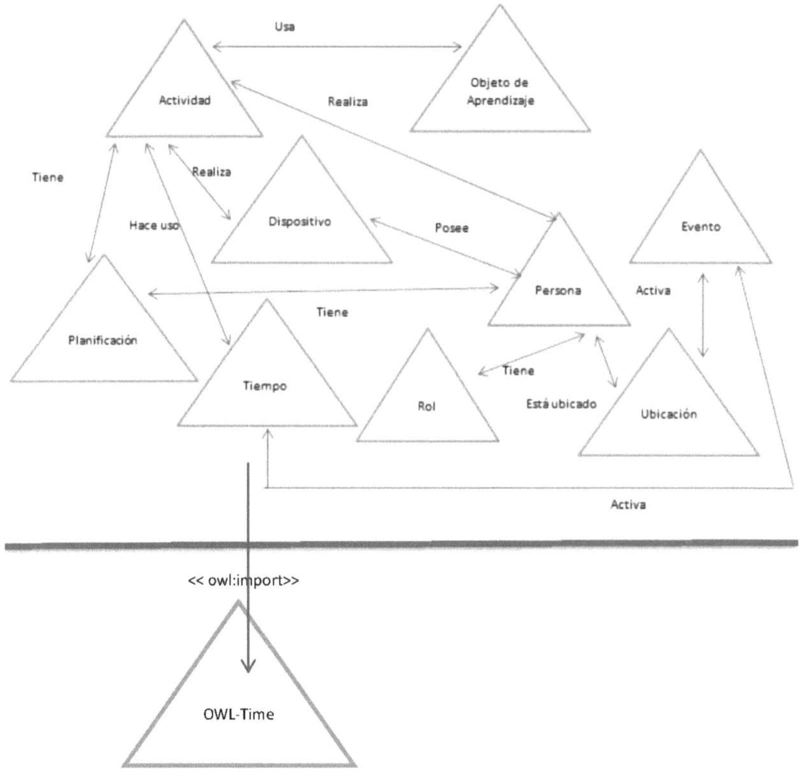

Figure 3 Integration of the OWL-Time ontology into the proposed Ontology Grid

The main entity of the OWL-Time ontology is *TemporalEntity* which is refined in two types: Instantaneous and Interval. A *TemporalEntity* has a start and an end. Also the ontology defines GeneralDateTimeDescription, DurationDescription and TemporalUnit. OWL-Time provides two alternative ways of representing time points TemporalDuration and xsd: dateTime.

- **Domain ontology search:**

The search for domain ontologies was based on the specification of requirements defined according to the NeOn methodology. For this purpose, semantic search engines such as Watson[1] , Semantic Web Search[2] , Swoogle[3] ,

---

[1] http://watson.kmi.open.ac.uk/WatsonWUI/

ProtegeWiki[4] were used. The following table lists the list of ontologies per domain

Table 4. Domain-related ontologies

Ontology	Organisation	URL
Person		
eBiquity Person	Stanford University, California	http://ebiquity.umbc.edu/ontology/person.owl
GUMO	Saarland University, Saarbrucken, Germany	www.gumo.org
Person	W3C org	https://www.w3.org/ns/person
FOAF	Dan Brickley and Libby Miller	http://xmlns.com/foaf/spec/
CoDAMOS	KU Leuven	https://distrinet.cs.kuleuven.be/projects/CoDAMoS/ontology/context.owl
Delivery Context	W3C	https://www.w3.org/TR/dcontology/
Device		
CoDAMOS	KU Leuven	https://distrinet.cs.kuleuven.be/projects/CoDAMoS/ontology/context.owl
Delivery Context	W3C	https://www.w3.org/TR/dcontology/
COBRA	Wang et at.	http://daml.umbc.edu/ontologies/cobra/0.4/personal-device
SOUPA	Chen et at.	http://ebiquity.umbc.edu/paper/html/id/165/The-SOUPA-Ontology-for-Pervasive-Computing
Location		
CoDAMOS	KU Leuven	https://distrinet.cs.kuleuven.be/projects/CoDAMoS/ontology/context.owl
Delivery Context	W3C	https://www.w3.org/TR/dcontology/
COBRA	Wang et at.	http://daml.umbc.edu/ontologies/cobra/0.4/location
SOUPA	Chen et at.	http://ebiquity.umbc.edu/paper/html/id/165/The-SOUPA-Ontology-for-Pervasive-Computing
Geo OWL	W3C	https://www.w3.org/2005/Incubator/geo/XGR-geo-ont-20071023/
Learning objects		
University	Butler, 2004	http://simile.mit.edu/repository/ontologie

---

[2] http://www.semanticwebsearch.com/query/
[3] http://swoogle.umbc.edu/2006/
[4] https://protegewiki.stanford.edu/wiki/Main_Page

Ontology		s/official/imsmd_educationalv1p2.rdfs
SUMO	ALH	http://reliant.teknowledge.com/DAML/S UMO.owl
LOM2OW L	Garcia et al., 2006	http://www.cc.uah.es/ie/ontologiaLOM2 OWL/LOM2OWL.owl
Event		
SOUPA	Chen et at.	http://ebiquity.umbc.edu/paper/html/id/1 65/The-SOUPA-Ontology-for-Pervasive-Computing
Event	Yves Raimond, Samer Abdallah	http://motools.sourceforge.net/event/even t.html
COBRA	Wang et at.	http://daml.umbc.edu/ontologies/cobra/0. 4/time-basic

2.9.3. Ontology comparison

After searching the ontologies by domains, the criteria of the NeOn methodology were applied to determine which ones to use and which ones to discard, for this purpose the following actions were carried out:

- Testing the scope and purpose of the DERO ontology with the candidate ontology
- Analyse the terms in the candidate ontology if they are similar to the ontology to be developed (Gómez and Lozano, 2005).

   Calculate the precision and scope of the terms of the candidate ontology to be reused with respect to the terms included in the competence questions defined for the new ontology (DERO).

- Analyse whether the candidate ontology answers the competency questions of the ontology requirements specification document.

The analysis for each of the sub-domains of the ontology network will be described below.

- Sub-domain Person

Table 5, Assessment of ontologies for reuse in the person sub-domain

Criterion	eBiquity Person	GUMO	Person	FOAF	CoDAMOS	Delivery Context
Similarity in scope	No	Partial	No	Yes	Partial	Yes
Objective Similar	No	Partial	No	Yes	Partial	No
Coverage of non-	No	No	Partial	Partial	Partial	No

functional requirements						
Coverage of functional requirements	Partial	No	Partial	Partial	Partial	Partial

Table 6 shows the candidate ontologies for reuse in the person subdomain. The ontologies that are closest to the ontology requirements specification document are FOAF and CoDAMos.

- Device subdomain
  Table 6, Valuation of ontologies for reuse in the device subdomain

Criterion	COBRA	SOUPA	CoDAMOS	Delivery Context
Similarity in scope	Partial	Partial	Partial	Yes
Objective Similar	Partial	Partial	Partial	No
Coverage of non-functional requirements	Partial	Partial	No	No
Coverage of functional requirements	Partial	No	No	Partial

Table 6 shows that the candidate ontologies that most closely match the DERO are COBRA and SOUPA.

- Sub-domain location
  Table 7, Valuation of ontologies for reuse in the location subdomain

Criterion	COBRA	SOUPA	CoDAMOS	Delivery Context	Geo OWL
Similarity in scope	Partial	Partial	Partial	Yes	Yes
Objective Similar	Partial	Partial	Partial	No	No
Coverage of non-functional requirements	Partial	No	No	No	No
Coverage of functional	Partial	No	Partial	Partial	Partial

requirements					

In table 7, it can be seen that the ontologies that come closest to the location subdomain are COBRA and CoDAMOS.

- Subdomain event
  Table 8, Valuation of ontologies for reuse in the event subdomain

Criterion	COBRA	SOUPA	Event
Similarity in scope	Partial	Partial	Partial
Objective Similar	Partial	No	No
Coverage of non-functional requirements	Partial	No	Partial
Coverage of functional requirements	Partial	No	No

In table 8, it can be seen that the ontologies that approach the event subdomain are COBRA and EVENT.

- Sub-domain learning objects
  Table 9, Assessment of ontologies for reuse in the sub-domain learning objects

Criterion	IMSPROJECT	SUMO	LOM2OWL
Similarity in scope	Partial	Partial	Partial
Objective Similar	Partial	Partial	Partial
Coverage of non-functional requirements	No	No	Partial
Coverage of functional requirements	Partial	No	Partial

In table 9, it can be seen that the ontologies that come closest to the location subdomain are IMSPROJECT and LOM2OWL.

2.9.4. Ontologies to be reused in this doctoral proposal

After comparing the different ontologies, two candidate ontologies per specific domain were chosen. The selected ontologies are:

a. Sub-domain Person
   i. FOAF
   ii. CODAMOS
b. Subdomain Device
   i. COBRA
   ii. SOUPA
c. Sub-domain Location
   i. COBRA
   ii. CODAMOS
d. Subdomain Event
   i. COBRA
   ii. EVENT
e. Sub-domain Learning Objects
   i. IMSPROJECT
   ii. LOM2OWL

The procedure for selecting the candidate ontology per domain is based on the analysis proposed by the NeOn methodology. The analysis consists of a set of criteria, divided into four categories: a) reusability cost, b) comprehensibility effort, c) integration effort and d) reliability. The criteria have weights, with a positive (+) or negative (-) assignment, the score has a range from 0 to 10. This weighting score will depend on the importance that the ontology development group assigns to the criteria. Each candidate ontology can be given a linguistic rating such as: unknown, low, medium and high. The transformation of the linguistic values obeys the following rule.

- Value = Unknown$\rightarrow$ Value=0
- Value = Low Value=1$\rightarrow$
- Value = Medium Value=2$\rightarrow$
- Value = High Value=3$\rightarrow$

After assigning the numerical values of the candidate ontologies in each of the criteria, the score calculation of the candidate ontologies is performed. The score is obtained by calculating the average weight, for positive and negative criteria, according to the following expressions:

$$Score\,ón_{i(+)} = \sum_{j(+)} ValueT_{i,j} \; x \; \frac{Weight_j}{\sum_j Weight_j} \quad \text{a) scoring with positive}$$

criteria

$$Score\,ón_{i(-)} = \sum_{j(-)} ValueT_{i,j} \; x \; \frac{Weight_j}{\sum_j Weight_j} \quad \text{b) scoring with negative}$$

criteria

Where

- i is a particular candidate ontology.
- $Score_{i(+)}$ corresponds to the candidate ontology 'i' for the set of criteria with a positive weight.
- $Score_{i(-)}$ corresponds to the candidate ontology 'i' for the set of criteria with a negative weight.
- j is a particular criterion, j(+) are the criteria with positive weight and j(-) are the criteria with negative weight.
- ValueTi, is the transformed numerical value for the criterion of j in ontology i.
- Pesoj is the numerical weight associated to criterion j.

The scoring to obtain the candidate ontology is achieved by the formula:

$$Puntuación_i = Puntuación_{(+i)} - Puntuación_{(-i)}$$

According to the above, the calculation of the different subdomains will be carried out. For example, table xx shows the calculation of the subdomain person, with the candidate ontologies FOAF and CoDAMos, as shown in table 10.

Table 10, Selection of ontologies for the subdomain Person.

Criterion	Weight	Values* Values* Values* Values* Values* Values* Values* Values* Values* Values* Values* Values	
		FOAF	CoDAMOS
Cost of reuse			
Economic cost of reuse	(-) 9	1	1
Time required for reuse	(-) 7	1	1
Compressive stress			
Quality documentation	(+) 8		
Availability of external expertise	(+) 7		

Code clarity	(+) 8		
Integration effort			
Adequacy of knowledge extraction	(+) 9		1
Adequacy of naming conventions	(+) 5		
Adequacy of the implementation language	(+) 7		
Knowledge conflicts	(-) 7		
Adaptation to the reasoner	(+) 7		
Need for bridging terms	(-) 6	1	1
Reliability			
Availability of evidence	(+) 8		1
Theoretical support	(+) 8		
Reputation of the development team	(+) 8		
Reliability of documentation	(+) 3		
Practical support	(+) 7		
Total		1,63	0,77

CHAPTER III: BUILDING OWL ONTOLOGIES IN PROTEGÉ

3. Requirements

Download from the official Stanford website
https://protect.stanford.edu/products.php#desktop-protects
Also download graphviz-2.38-win32.msi; from the following link:
https://www2.graphviz.org/Packages/stable/windows/10/msbuild/Release/Win3
2/

3.1. Configuration

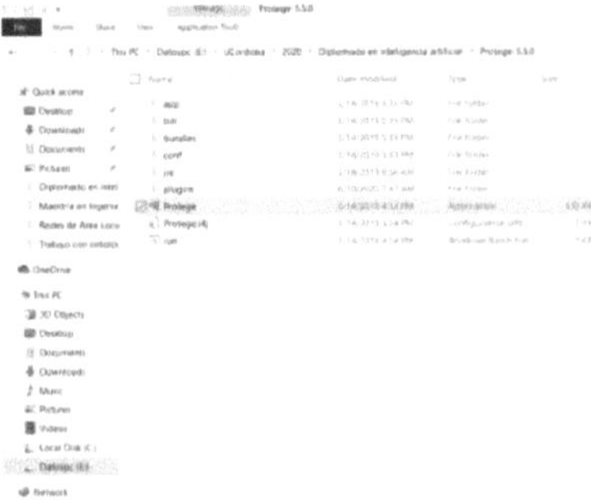

CONSTRUCCIÓN DE ONTOLOGÍAS OWL EN PROTEGÉ

Vaya a la opción reasoner, configure

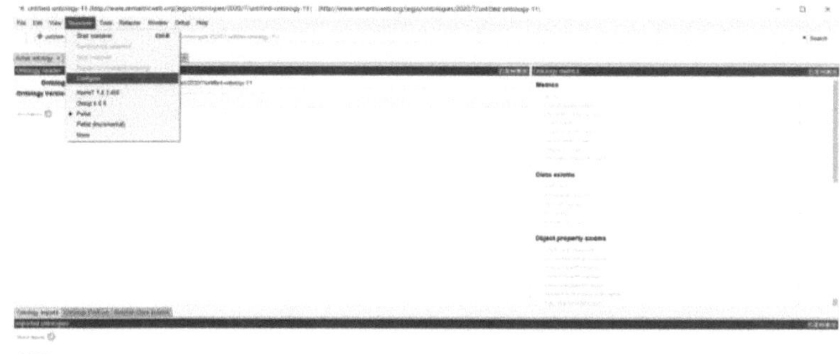

CONSTRUCCIÓN DE ONTOLOGÍAS OWL EN PROTEGÉ

Selecccione la pestaña OWLViz y ubique la ruta donde se instalo Graphviz2.38; por lo general queda instalado en esta ruta: C:\Program Files (x86)\Graphviz2.38\bin\dot.exe

Esta función permite visualizar la ontología (ver fig. 2)

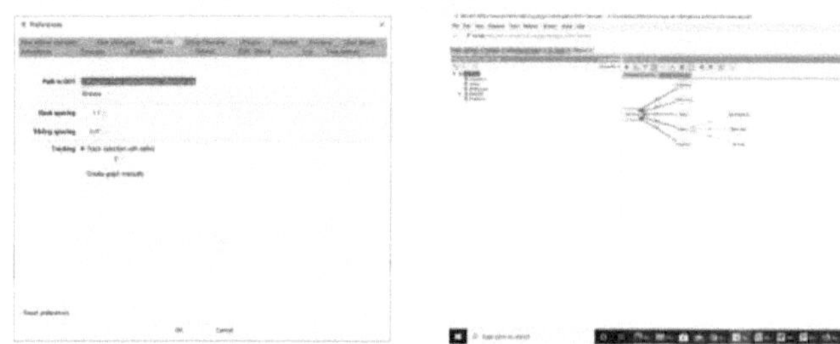

Fig. 1. Configuración Graphviz2.38

Fig. 2. Visualización Ontología

CONSTRUCCIÓN DE ONTOLOGÍAS OWL EN PROTEGÉ

En la opción Windows , Tabs

active: Classes, Object properties, Data properties, OWLViz

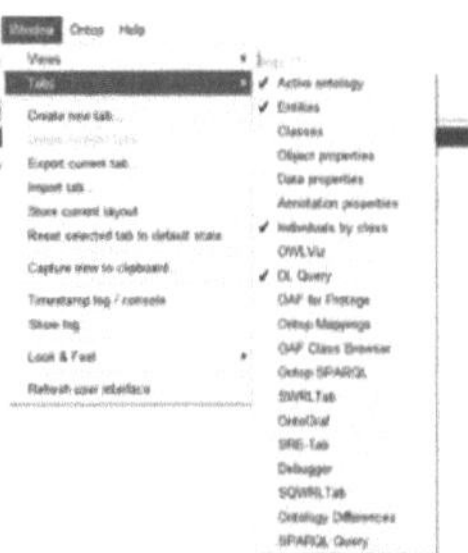

CONSTRUCCIÓN DE ONTOLOGÍAS OWL EN PROTEGÉ

Lo primero que hay que hacer al momento de crear la ontologías es asignar una IRI (Internationalized Resource Identifier)

Para este ejemplo asigne el siguiente IRI:

http://www.semanticweb.org/jegjo/ontologies/Myontology

CONSTRUCCIÓN DE ONTOLOGÍAS OWL EN PROTEGÉ

A continuación en el menú File Save as

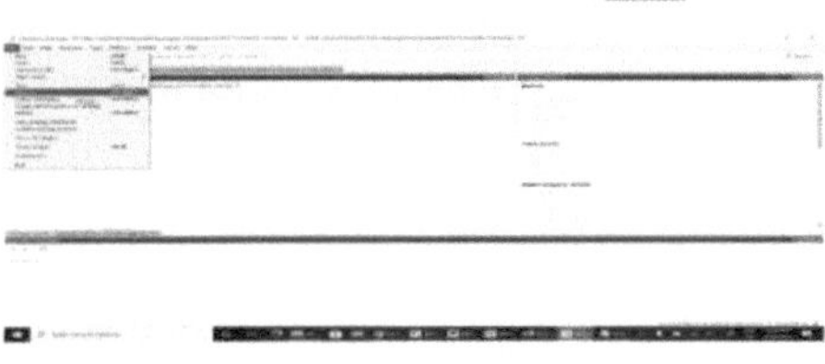

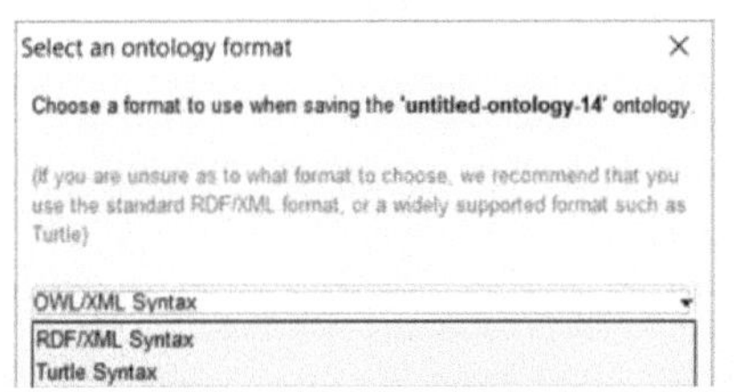

Seleccione la opción OWL/XML, Posteriormente haga clic en OK

CONSTRUCCIÓN DE ONTOLOGÍAS OWL EN PROTEGÉ

Representaremos el siguiente problema en una ontología llamada University – Clases y Relaciones; Dominios y Rangos

CONSTRUCCIÓN DE ONTOLOGÍAS OWL EN PROTEGÉ

Propiedades de las clases

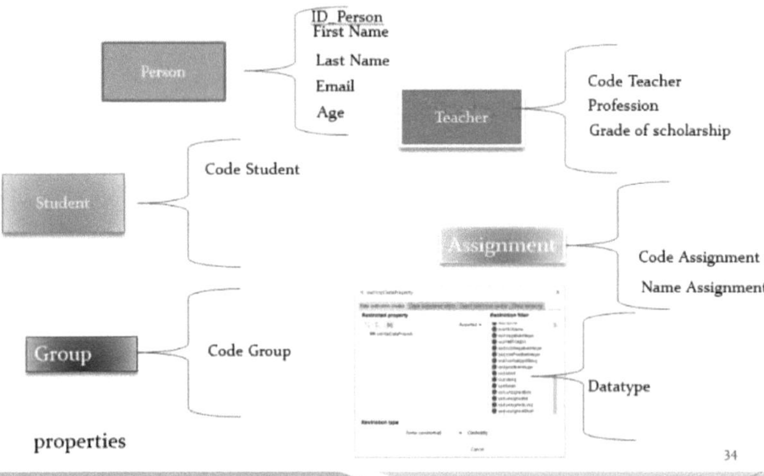

CONSTRUCCIÓN DE ONTOLOGÍAS OWL EN PROTEGÉ

- A continuación active las siguientes pestañas en la opción Windows, tabs: Active Ontology, Entities, Classes, Object Properties, Data Properties, Indivual by Class, OWLViz, DLQuery, Ontograph

3.2. *Creating the ontology*

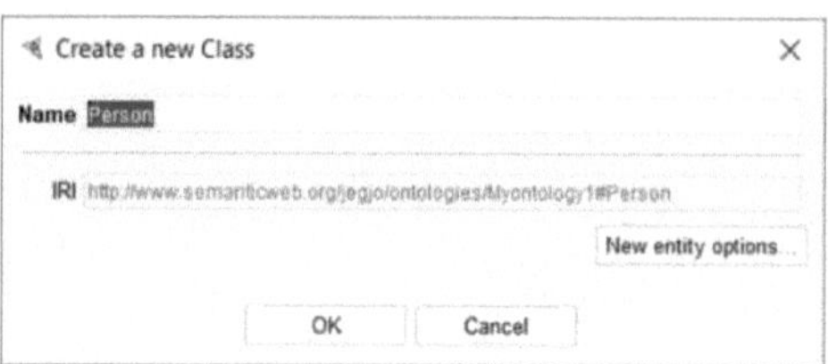

CONSTRUCCIÓN DE ONTOLOGÍAS OWL EN PROTEGÉ

- Se verá la primera clase creada

CONSTRUCCIÓN DE ONTOLOGÍAS OWL EN PROTEGÉ

- Como se observa en la figura las clases Student y Teacher, son subclases de la clase Persona

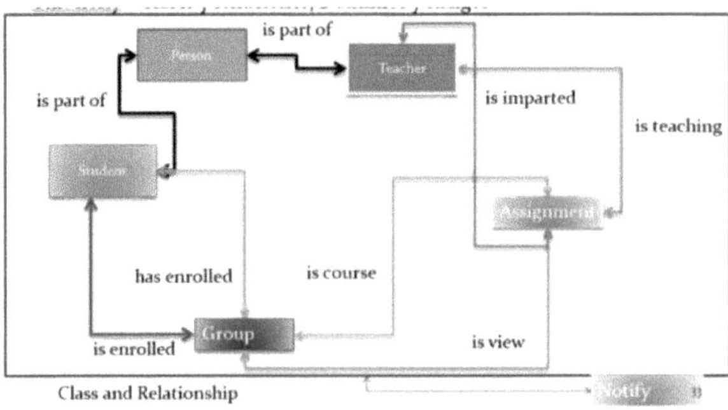

CONSTRUCCIÓN DE ONTOLOGÍAS OWL EN PROTEGÉ

- Debajo de la clase Person, se creará las clases Student y Teacher, haciendo clic en add sub classes

CONSTRUCCIÓN DE ONTOLOGÍAS OWL EN PROTEGÉ

- Debajo de la clase owl:Thing, crear las clases Group, Assignment y Notify

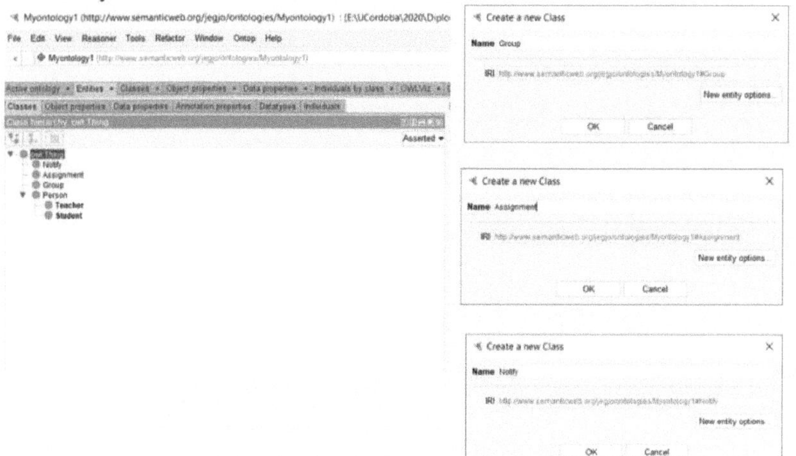

3.4. Building relationships

CONSTRUCCIÓN DE ONTOLOGÍAS OWL EN PROTEGÉ

- A continuación haga clic en la pestaña Object Properties, esto con el objeto de definir las relaciones entre las clases. Ubique el puntero del mouse en la opción owl:topObjectProperty. Luego haga clic en la opción add sub property

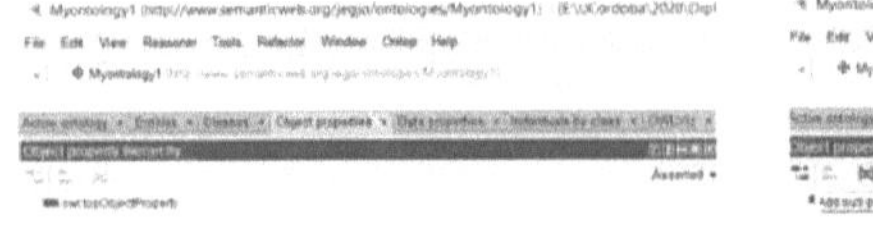
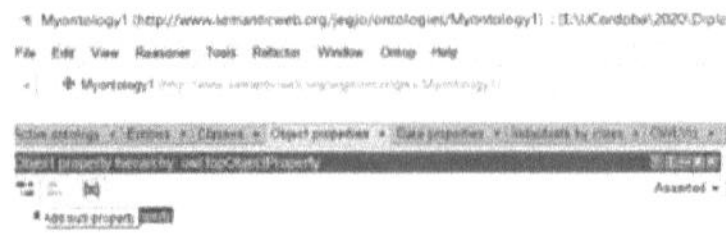

CONSTRUCCIÓN DE ONTOLOGÍAS OWL EN PROTEGÉ

- Escriba el nombre de la propiedades: is_Enrolled, has_Enrolled, is_View, is_Course, is_Imparted, is_Teaching

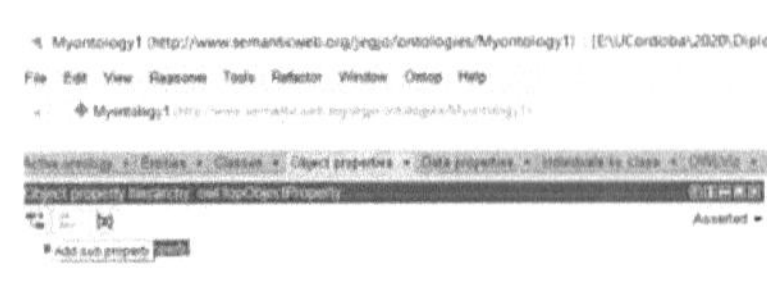
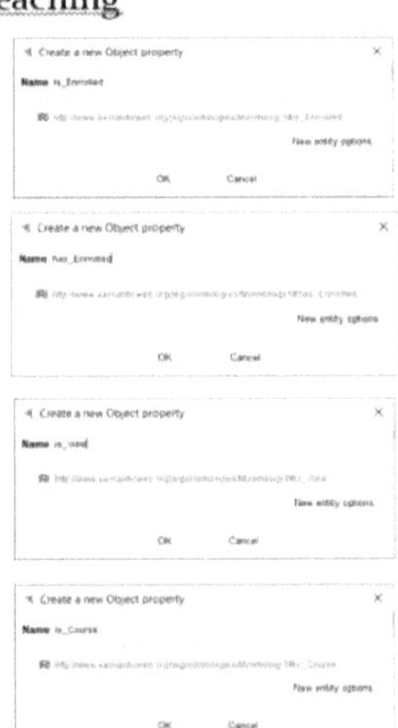

CONSTRUCCIÓN DE ONTOLOGÍAS OWL EN PROTEGÉ

- Haga clic en la opción <u>Domain Intersection</u>

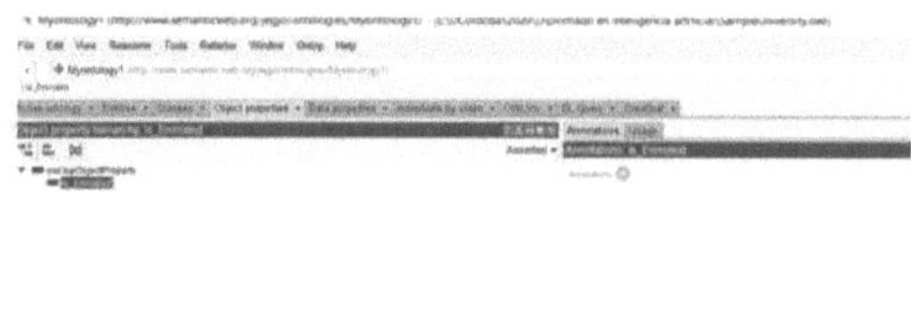

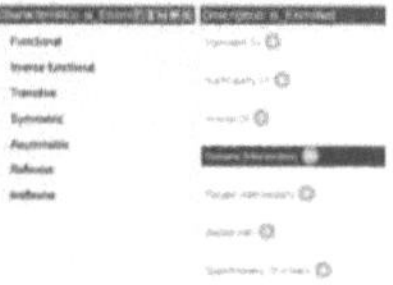

3.5. *Creating relationships*

CONSTRUCCIÓN DE ONTOLOGÍAS OWL EN PROTEGÉ

- Tome como referencia las relaciones (Propiedades), que se observan en la figura

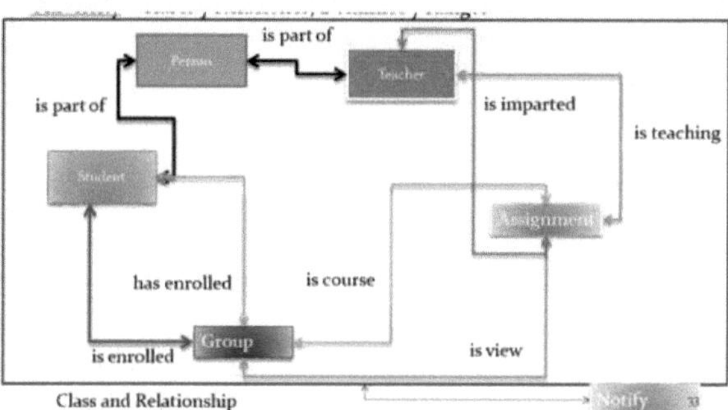

- Propiedades Inversas, por ejemplo la inversa de is_Enrolled es has_Enrolled, Clic en inverse Of y seleccione la propiedad que quiere asociar y haga clic en OK

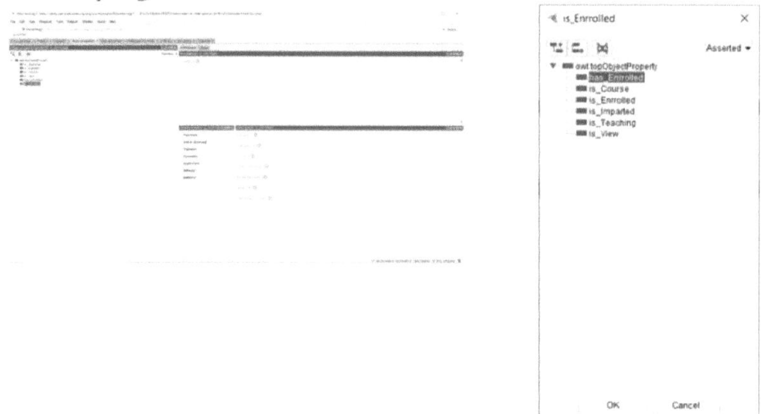

3.6. Defining properties

CONSTRUCCIÓN DE ONTOLOGÍAS OWL EN PROTEGÉ

- A Continuación se definirán los Data properties

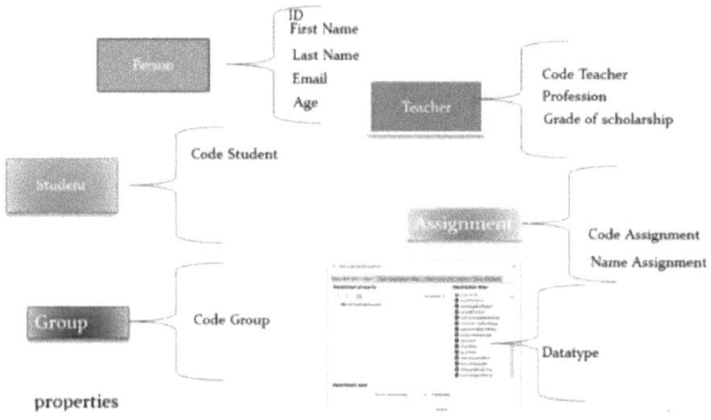

- Haga clic en la pestaña Data property, luego haga clic en owl:dataproperty, luego clic en la opción add sub property

3.7. Defining data types

CONSTRUCCIÓN DE ONTOLOGÍAS OWL EN PROTEGÉ

- Luego escoja el tipo de datos que va a utilizar para representar. Haga clic en la opción Ranges, luego clic en la pestaña Build in datatypes y seleccione el tipo de dato. Luego haga clic en OK. Haga la misma operación con todos los datos.

CONSTRUCCIÓN DE ONTOLOGÍAS OWL EN PROTEGÉ

- Al final tendremos algo como esto

Ustedes pueden seleccionar el datatype
Se recomienda usar xsd:string, debido a que es más fácil parsear en los lenguajes de programación

3.9. *Defining instances*

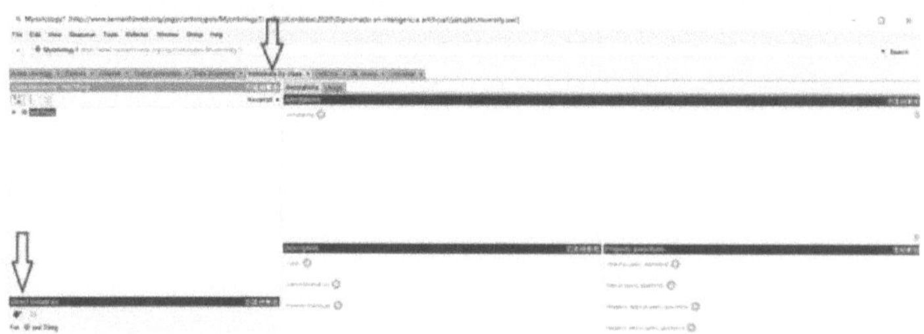

CONSTRUCCIÓN DE ONTOLOGÍAS OWL EN PROTEGÉ

- A continuación haga clic en la pestaña Individuals by class, esto permitirá crear las instancias dependiendo de cada clase. Luego haga clic Direct instances

CONSTRUCCIÓN DE ONTOLOGÍAS OWL EN PROTEGÉ

- A se describirán en la tabla las instancias de las diferentes clases Students

Id_Student	First Name	Last Name	Age	Email
Stdo001	Jorge	Perez	18	jperez@gmail.com
Stdo002	Sebastian	Lopez	16	jlopez@gmail.com
Stdo003	Carlos	Castillo	21	ccastillo@gmail.com
Stdo004	Juan	Riquelme	22	jriquelme@gmail.com
Stdo005	Adriana	Bustamante	19	abustamante@gmail.com
Stdo006	Juan	Corrales	23	jcorrales@gmail.com
Stdo007	Marcela	Berrio	20	mberrio@gmail.com
Stdo008	Gabriel	Ochoa	18	gochoa@gmail.com
Stdo009	Dayana	Rosse	22	drosse@gmail.com
Stdo010	Cristian	Tafur	20	ctafur@gmail.com
Stdo011	Alirio	Montalvo	21	cmontalvo@gmail.com
Stdo012	Marcos	Ferreira	23	mferreira@gmail.com

- A se describirán en la tabla las instancias de las diferentes clases

Teacher

Id_Student	First Name	Last Name	Age	Email
Teach0001	Velssy	Hernandez	50	vhernandez@gmail.com
Teach 0002	Pedro	Guevara	36	pguevara@gmail.com
Teach 0003	Samir	Castano	38	scastano@gmail.com
Teach 0004	Harold	Bula	51	jbula@gmail.com
Teach 0005	Daniel	Salas	52	dsalas@gmail.com

Group

Id_Group	Name	Location
Grp0001	GrpTelematica1	Bloque 43
Grp0002	GrpRedes Locales1	Bloque 43
Grp0003	GrpBases de Datos1	Bloque 16

Assignment

Id_Asignment	Name	Semester
Asg0001	Telematica	VII
Asg0002	Redes Locales	IX
Asg0003	Bases de Datos	VI

- A continuación haga clic en la pestaña Individuals by class, esto permitirá crear las instancias dependiendo de cada clase. Luego haga clic Direct instances

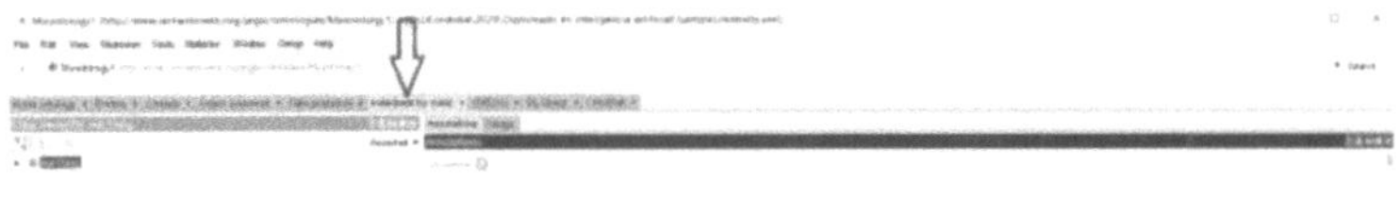

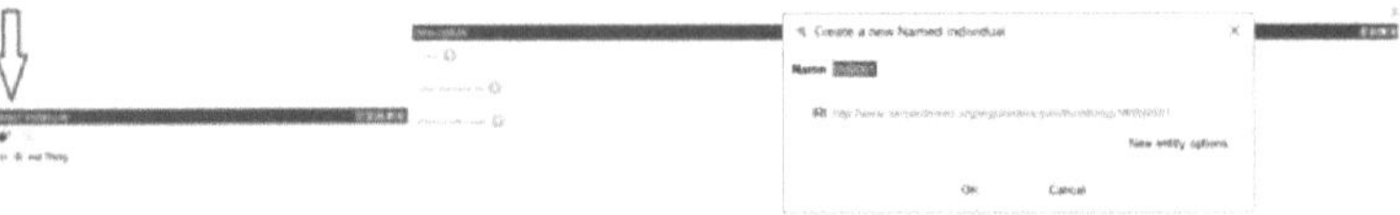

CONSTRUCCIÓN DE ONTOLOGÍAS OWL EN PROTEGÉ

- Al final el listado de instancias debe verse así:

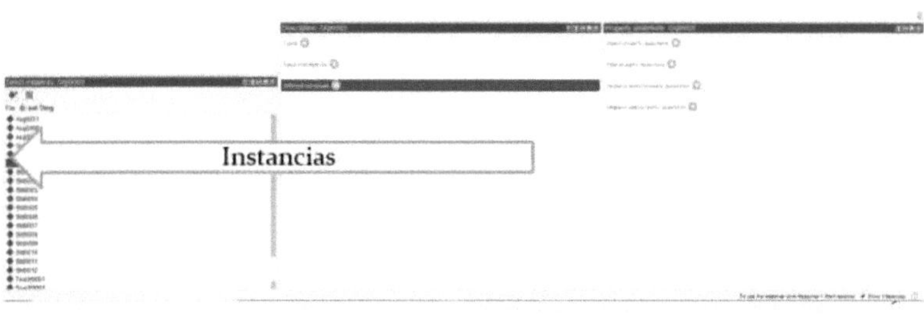

CONSTRUCCIÓN DE ONTOLOGÍAS OWL EN PROTEGÉ

- A continuación llenamos la información de las distintas instancias, haciendo clic en la opción Data property assertions

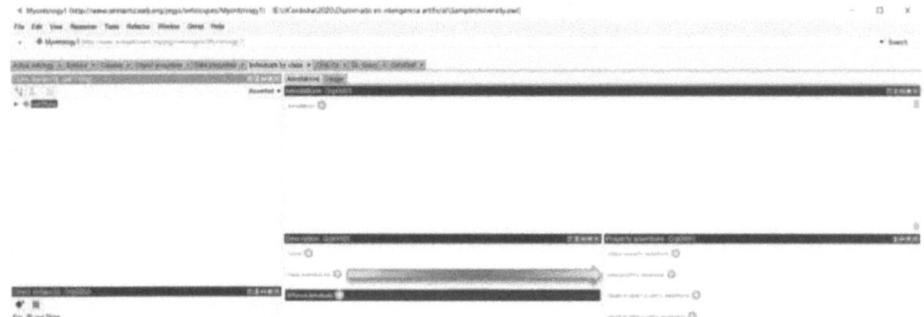

CONSTRUCCIÓN DE ONTOLOGÍAS OWL EN PROTEGÉ

- Se escoge la propiedad a la cual se quiere adicionar, en frente se le asigna el valor y en la opción Type seleccione la opción xsd:string, clic en OK

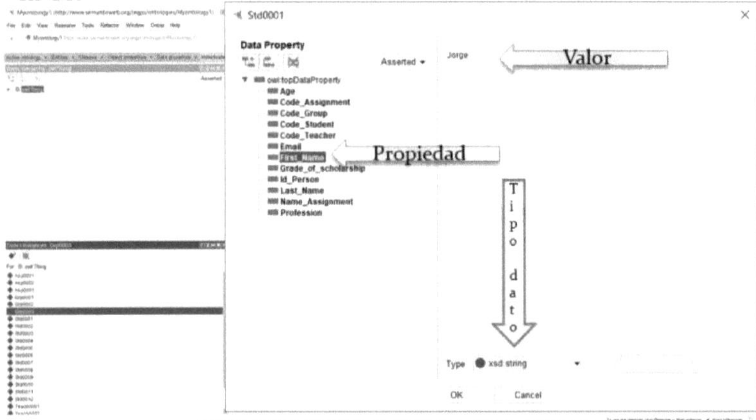

CONSTRUCCIÓN DE ONTOLOGÍAS OWL EN PROTEGÉ

- En la figura se observan los datos correspondiente para la instancia Std0001 con sus respectivos datos. Este mismo procedimiento se repite para todas las instancias.

- En la tabla siguiente se asignarán los estudiantes a un grupo. De esta forma se establece la relación directa entre Student y Group, en este caso la relación (Object Property) se llamará is_Enrrolled y su inversa has_Enrrolled

Id_Student	First Name	Last Name	Age	Email	Group
Stdo001	Jorge	Perez	18	jperez@gmail.com	Grp0001
Stdo002	Sebastian	Lopez	16	jlopez@gmail.com	Grp0001
Stdo003	Carlos	Castillo	21	ccastillo@gmail.com	Grp0001
Stdo004	Juan	Riquelme	22	lriquelme@gmail.com	Grp0001
Stdo005	Adriana	Bustamante	19	abustamante@gmail.com	Grp0001
Stdo006	Juan	Corrales	23	jcorrales@gmail.com	Grp0002
Stdo007	Marcela	Berrio	20	mberrio@gmail.com	Grp0002
Stdo008	Gabriel	Ochoa	18	gochoa@gmail.com	Grp0002
Stdo009	Dayana	Rosse	22	drosse@gmail.com	Grp0002
Stdo010	Cristian	Tafur	20	ctafur@gmail.com	Grp0003
Stdo011	Alirio	Montalvo	21	amontalvo@gmail.com	Grp0003
Stdo012	Marcos	Ferreira	23	mferreira@gmail.com	Grp0003

- A continuación se asociaran las relaciones entre las instancias de las diferentes clases.

Relaciones entre estudiante y grupo. Haga clic en Object property assertions.

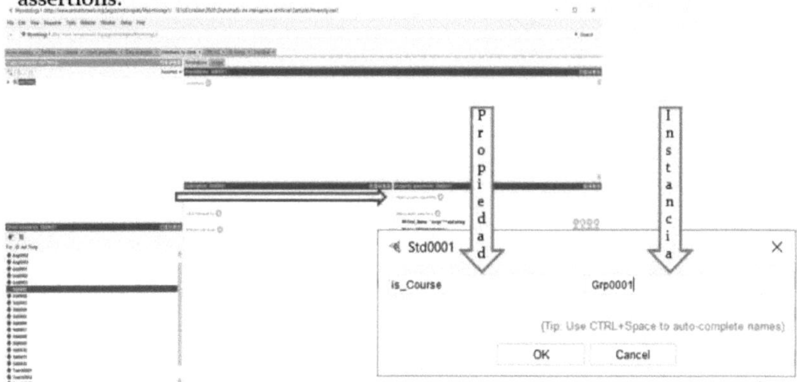

CONSTRUCCIÓN DE ONTOLOGÍAS OWL EN PROTEGÉ

- Este mismo procedimiento se repite para todas las instancias y las propiedades Student

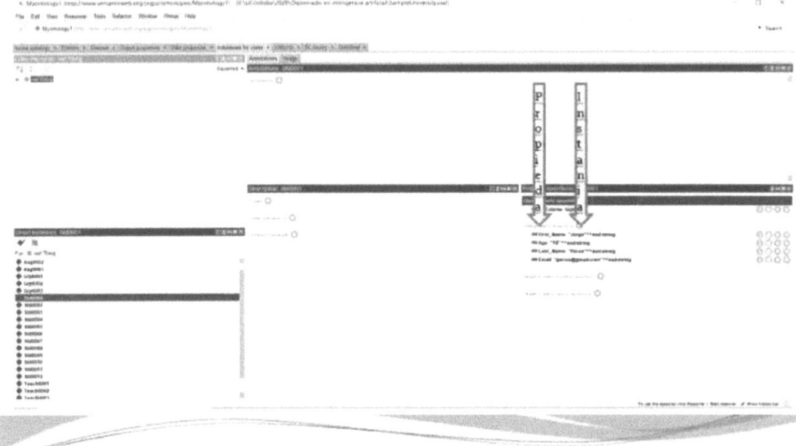

CONSTRUCCIÓN DE ONTOLOGÍAS OWL EN PROTEGÉ

- En la tabla siguiente se asignarán los docentes a un grupo. De esta forma se establece la relación directa entre Teacher y Asignment, en este caso la relación (Object Property) se llamará is_Imparte y su inversa is_Teaching

Teacher

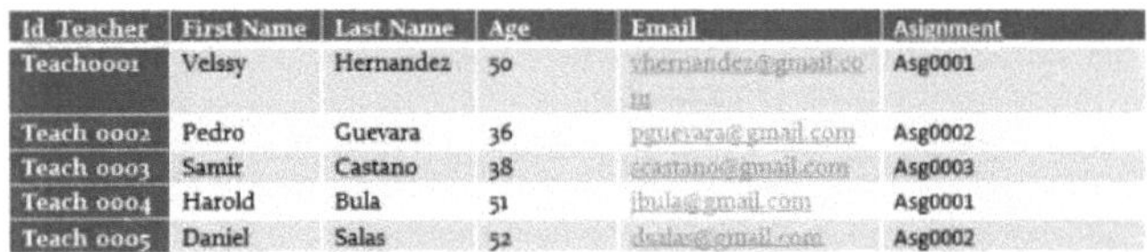

Id_Teacher	First Name	Last Name	Age	Email	Asignment
Teach0001	Velssy	Hernandez	50	vhernandez@gmail.com	Asg0001
Teach 0002	Pedro	Guevara	36	pguevara@gmail.com	Asg0002
Teach 0003	Samir	Castano	38	ecastano@gmail.com	Asg0003
Teach 0004	Harold	Bula	51	jbula@gmail.com	Asg0001
Teach 0005	Daniel	Salas	52	dsalas@gmail.com	Asg0002

CONSTRUCCIÓN DE ONTOLOGÍAS OWL EN PROTEGÉ

- Este mismo procedimiento se repite para todas las instancias y las propiedades de Teacher

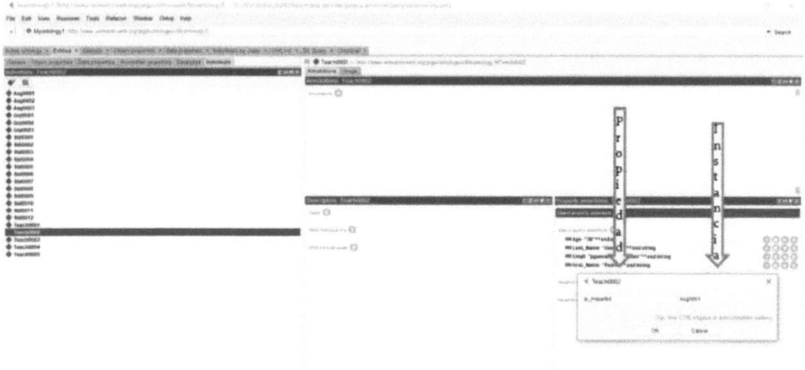

CONSTRUCCIÓN DE ONTOLOGÍAS OWL EN PROTEGÉ

- Este mismo procedimiento se repite para todas las instancias y las propiedades de Teacher

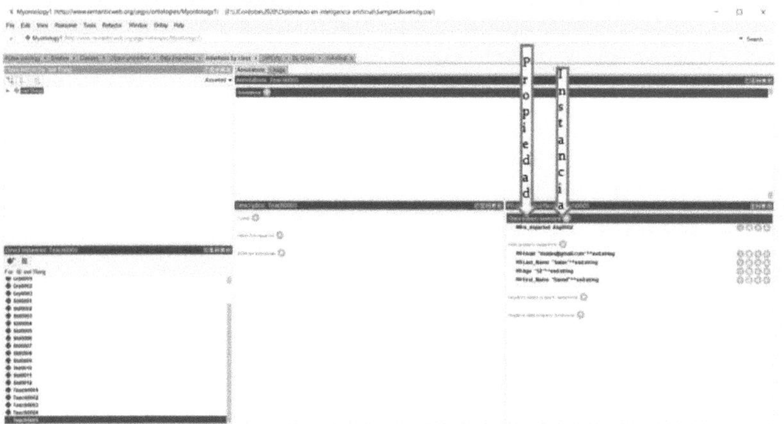

CONSTRUCCIÓN DE ONTOLOGÍAS OWL EN PROTEGÉ

- En la tabla siguiente se asignarán los docentes a un grupo. De esta forma se establece la relación directa entre Group y Asignment, en este caso la relación (Object Property) se llamará is_Course y su inversa is_View

Group

Id_Group	Name	Location	Id_Asignment
Grp0001	GrpTelematica1	Bloque 43	Asg0001
Grp0002	GrpRedes Locales1	Bloque 43	Asg0002
Grp0003	GrpBases de Datos1	Bloque 16	Asg0003

CONSTRUCCIÓN DE ONTOLOGÍAS OWL EN PROTEGÉ

- Este mismo procedimiento se repite para todas las instancias y las propiedades de Group

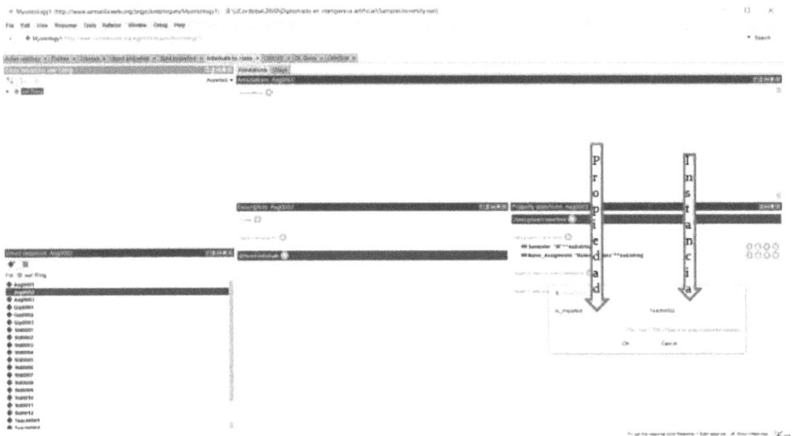

CONSTRUCCIÓN DE ONTOLOGÍAS OWL EN PROTEGÉ

- En la figura se observa la relación entre asignatura y grupo

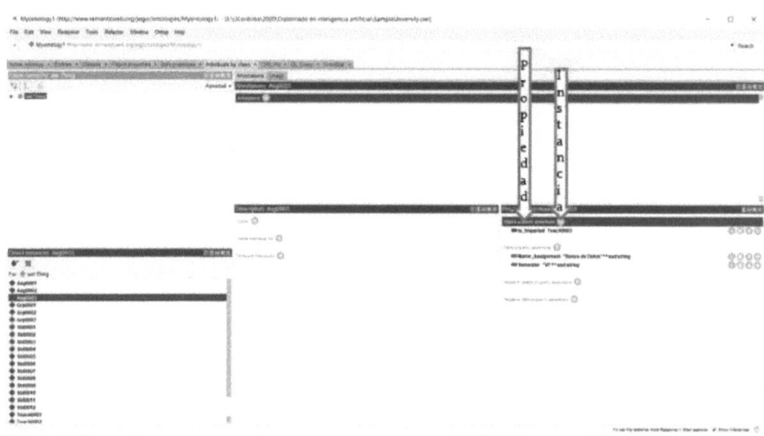

CONSTRUCCIÓN DE ONTOLOGÍAS OWL EN PROTEGÉ

- A continuación haga clic en la pestaña ontograf. Esto permitirá visualizar la ontología con las clases y sus respectivas relaciones

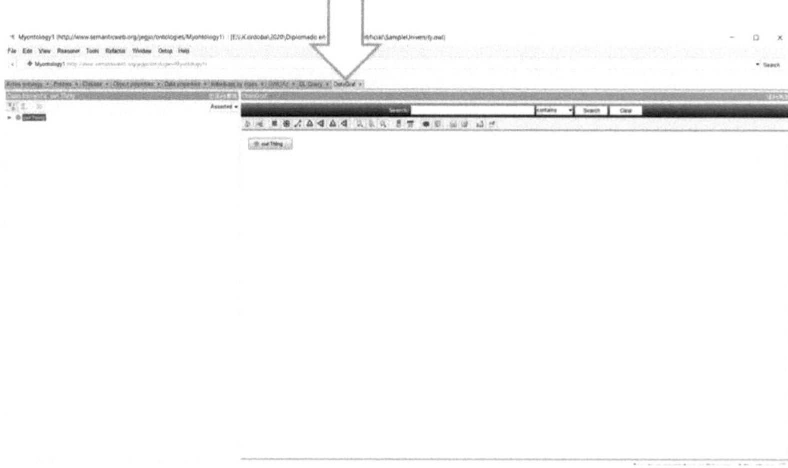

CONSTRUCCIÓN DE ONTOLOGÍAS OWL EN PROTEGÉ

- A continuación haga doble clic en la opción owl:thing que se encuentra señalado con la flecha

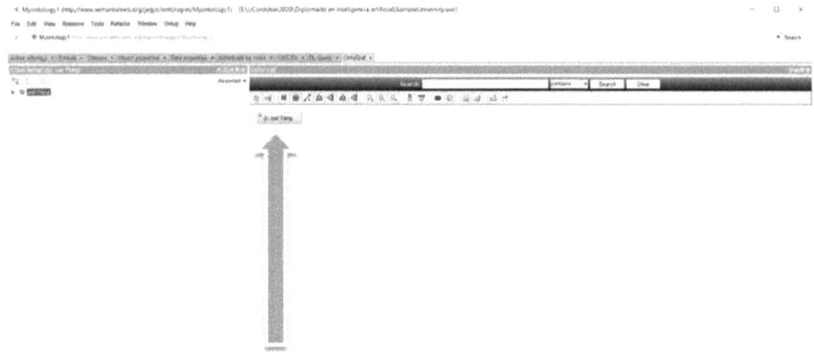

CONSTRUCCIÓN DE ONTOLOGÍAS OWL EN PROTEGÉ

- Aparecen en Ontograf, las clase principal owl:thing y las subclases que se definieron para el problema en cuestión.

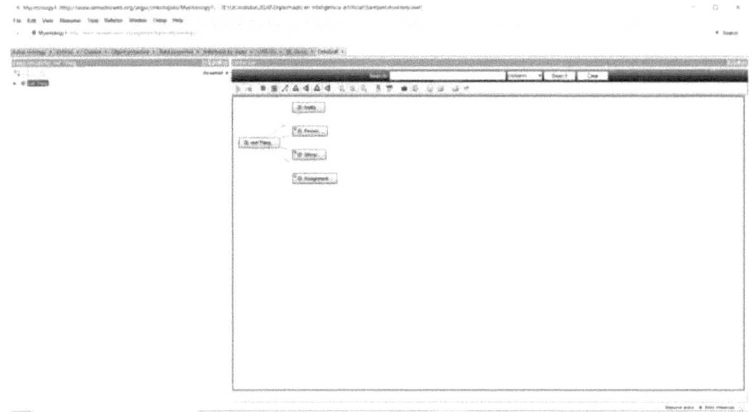

CONSTRUCCIÓN DE ONTOLOGÍAS OWL EN PROTEGÉ

- Aparecen en Ontograf, las clase principal owl:thing y las subclases que se definieron para el problema en cuestión. Note que las clases Persona, Group y Assignment tienen un signo +, haga clic encima de cada uno de ellas. Primero empiece con la clase persona.

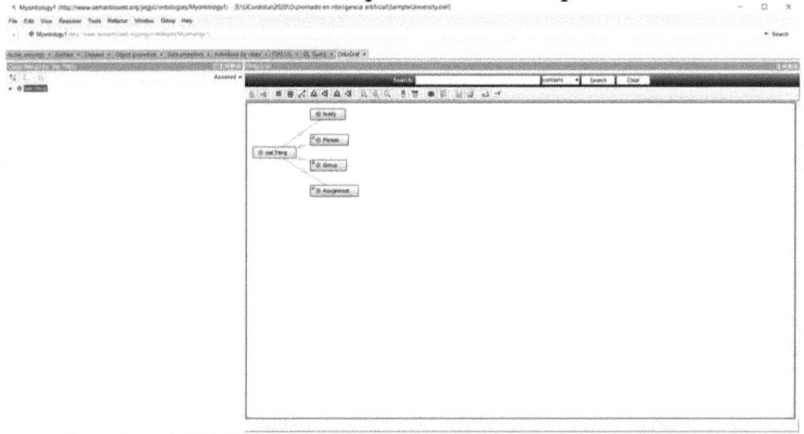

CONSTRUCCIÓN DE ONTOLOGÍAS OWL EN PROTEGÉ

- De la clase persona se derivan las subclases Student y Teacher. Haga clic en el singo + en la clase Student.

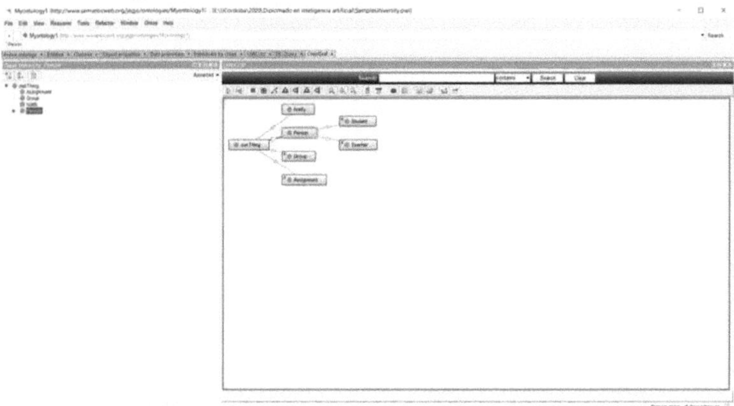

CONSTRUCCIÓN DE ONTOLOGÍAS OWL EN PROTEGÉ

- Como se puede observar en la figura se despliegan las instancias de la clases persona junto con las relaciones entre Student y Group. Si señala con el puntero del mouse las flechas que comunican a Student y Group, se visualizan las relaciones is_Enrolled y has_Enrolled.

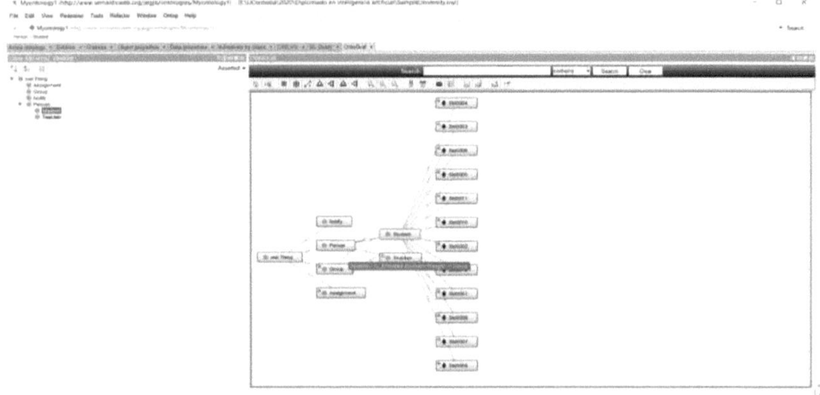

CONSTRUCCIÓN DE ONTOLOGÍAS OWL EN PROTEGÉ

- A continuación arrastre la clase Teacher hacia la parte derecha en un lugar despejado y haga doble clic en el signo +, debe aparecer las relaciones y la instancias de esta clase. Repita este mismo procedimiento para las clases Group y Assignment.

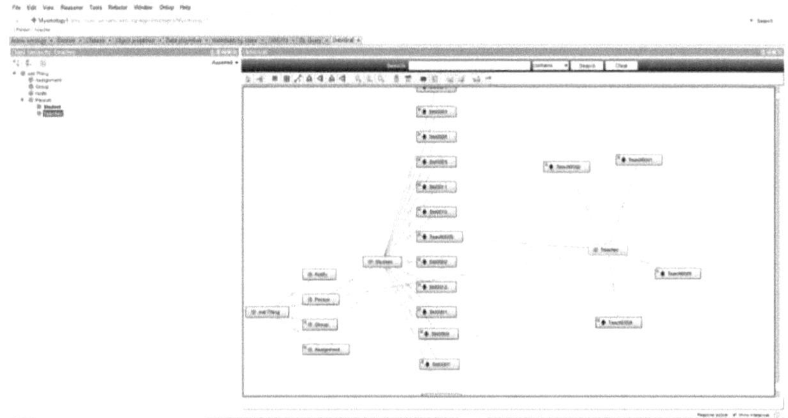

CONSTRUCCIÓN DE ONTOLOGÍAS OWL EN PROTEGÉ

- A continuación haga clic en la pestana Classes., luego vaya al menú Windows, view, Ontologyview, Rules. Ubique la opción en la parte señala por la flecha

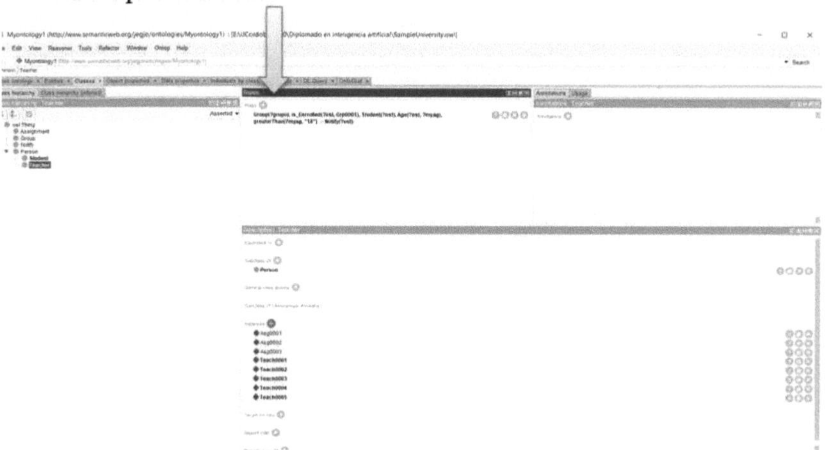

CONSTRUCCIÓN DE ONTOLOGÍAS OWL EN PROTEGÉ

- A continuación crearemos la siguiente regla:
- Group(?grupo), is_Enrolled(?est, Grp0001), Student(?est) -> Notify(?est)

CONSTRUCCIÓN DE ONTOLOGÍAS OWL EN PROTEGÉ

- A continuación haga clic en el menú <u>reasoner</u>, <u>Synchronize reasoner</u>, luego haga clic en la parte izquierda en la clase <u>Notify</u>. La flecha señala las instancias que cumplen con esa regla

CHAPTER IV: PROGRAMMING ONTOLOGIES IN JAVA AND APACHE JENA

Apache Jena is a free and open source Java framework for creating semantic and linked data web applications. The framework is composed of different APIs that interact together to process RDF data. Figure 1 shows the framework architecture.

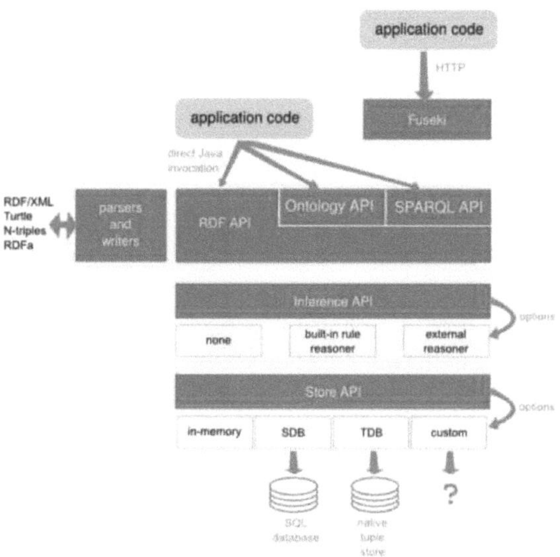

Figure 1. Apache Jena framework architecture (source https://jena.apache.org/getting_started/index.html)

Figure 2 shows the architecture of the semantic Web protocol stack.

Semantic Web Stack

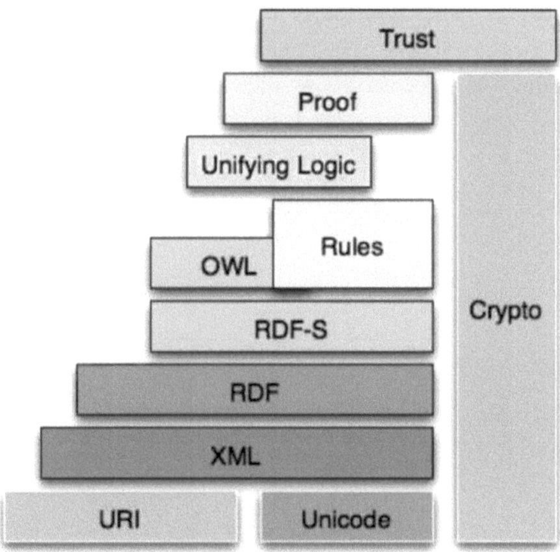

Figure 2. semantic web protocol stack

(RuleML)

- It is an effort to standardise the rules of inference.

- RuleML is a markup language for publishing and sharing rule bases worldwide.

Web.

- The focus is on the interoperability of rules between

industry standards.

- RuleML creates a hierarchy of rules

sub-languages in XML, RDF and OWL, e.g. SWRL.

What is SWRL?

- SWRL is an acronym for Semantic Web Rule.

- SWRL is intended to be the rules language of the Semantic Web.

- SWRL includes a high-level abstract syntax for Horn Rules.

- All rules are expressed in terms of OWL concepts (classes, properties, individuals).

Characteristics SWRL

- W3C presentation in 2004:

http://www.w3.org/Submission/SWRL/

- Rules stored as part of the ontology

- Broader tool support: Bossam, R2ML, Hoolet, Pellet, KAON2, RacerPro, SWRLTab

- Can work with reasoners.

Example of rules in SWRL

> **Rule: Group(?group), has_Enrolled(Grp01, ? est), Student(? est)-> Notification(? est)**

> **Rule: Group(?group), has_Enrolled(Grp01, ? est), Student(? est), hasAge(? est, ?age), greaterThan(?age, 18) -> Notification(? est)**

> **Rule: Group(? grupo), is_Enrolled(? est, Grp0001), Student(? est), Age(? est, ? xage), greaterThan(? xage, "15") -> Notify(? est)**

> **Rule: Group(? grupo), is_Enrolled(? est, Grp0001), Student(? est), is_A_Student(? est, ? grd), Grading(Gra00001), has_Grading(? grd, ? assg), Assignment(? assg) -> Notify(? est)**

SPARQL query language for RDF

RDF is a tagged and directed graph data format for representing information on the Web. RDF is often used to represent, among other things, personal information, social networks, metadata about digital artefacts, as well as to provide a means of integration over disparate information sources. This specification defines the syntax and semantics of the SPARQL query language for RDF.

Example queries

```
PREFIX owl: <http://www.w3.org/2002/07/owl#>
 PREFIX rdf: <http://www.w3.org/1999/02/22-rdf-syntax-ns#>
            PREFIX rdfs: <http://www.w3.org/2000/01/rdf-schema#>
            PREFIX                                              ROSCC:
<http://www.semanticweb.org/jegjo/ontologies/Myontology1#>
 SELECT ? first_name ? last_name ?age

            WHERE {
 Student ROSCC:First_Name ? first_name.
 Student ROSCC:Last_Name ? last_name.
  ?Student ROSCC:Age ?age.
            }
```

4.1. Ontology query development in Netbeans

First download the following information from the links:
1. Netbeans
   https://www.apache.org/dyn/closer.cgi/netbeans/netbeans/12.1/Apache-NetBeans-12.1-bin-windows-x64.exe

2. In the shared folder you will download the SampleUniversity4.OWL file and download the complete lib folder.

https://drive.google.com/drive/u/1/folders/1uwIoGBVNHJR5ea2_bxPcCH678Q
bvMc-a

Once Netbeans 8.2 is installed, follow the instructions below:

Steps:
1. Run Netbeans
2. As shown in figure 3, click on the menu File -> New Projet

Figure 3. Netbeans project creation
3. Choose the option Java -> Java Application, as shown in figure 4.

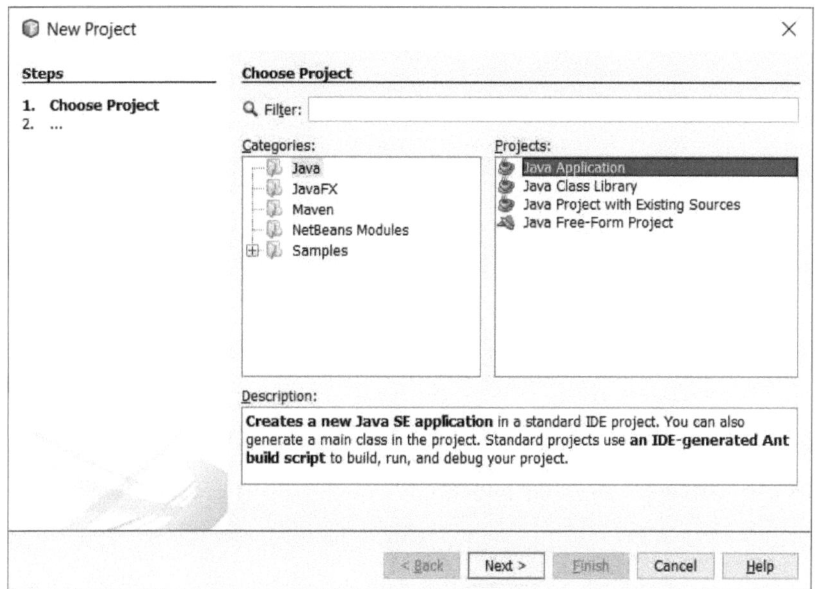

Figure 4. Netbeans project creation, application type selection

4. Type in Project Name: Firstontology, see figure 5.

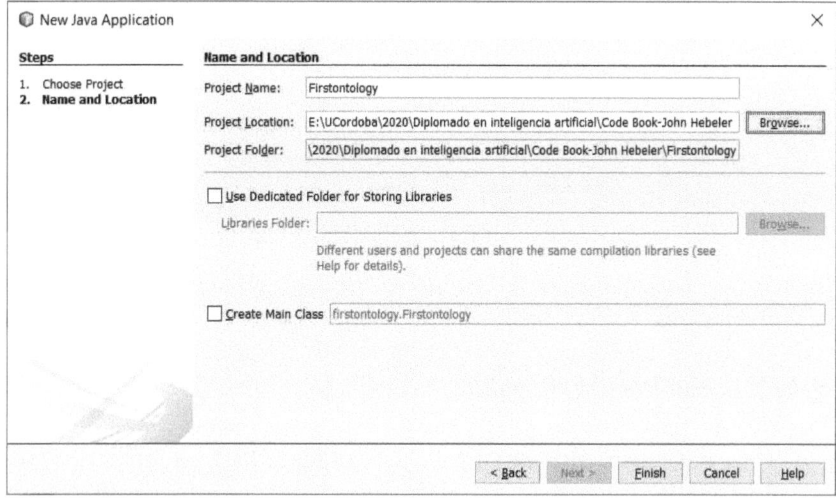

Figure 5. Definition of the project name

5. Select the destination folder where the project will be stored, see figure 6 and 7.

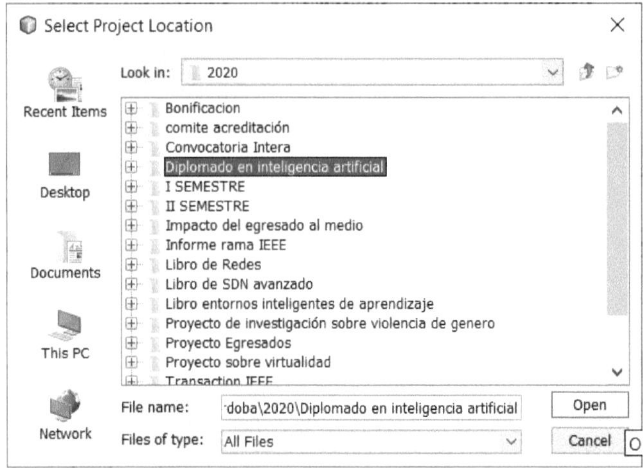

Figure 6. Location to save the project

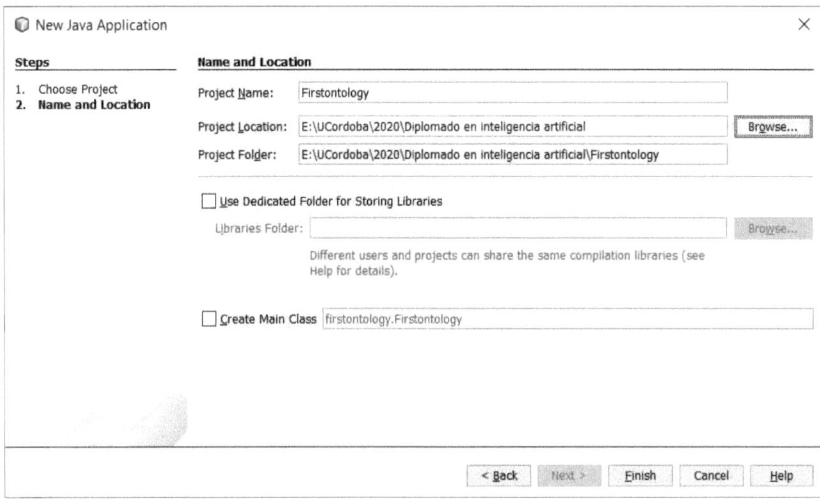

Figure 7. Location to save the project

6. Once the project is created, right click on Source Package -> New -> Java
    Package, see figure 8.

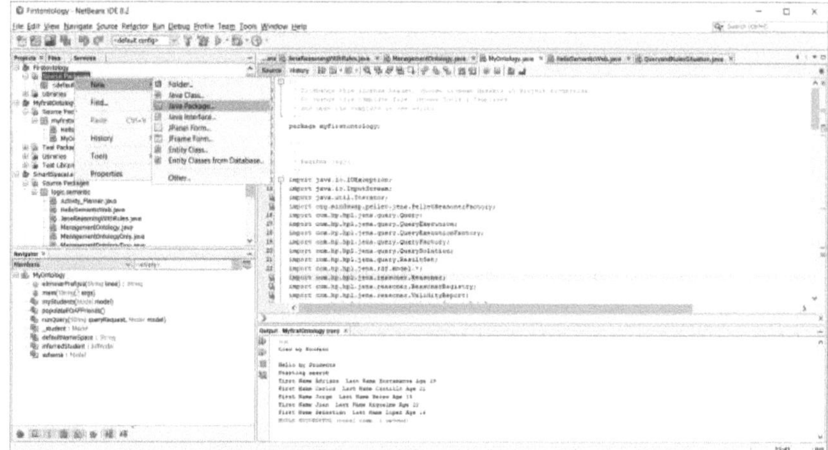

Figure 8. Creation of the package

7. In Package Name type com.logic, then Finish, see figure 9.

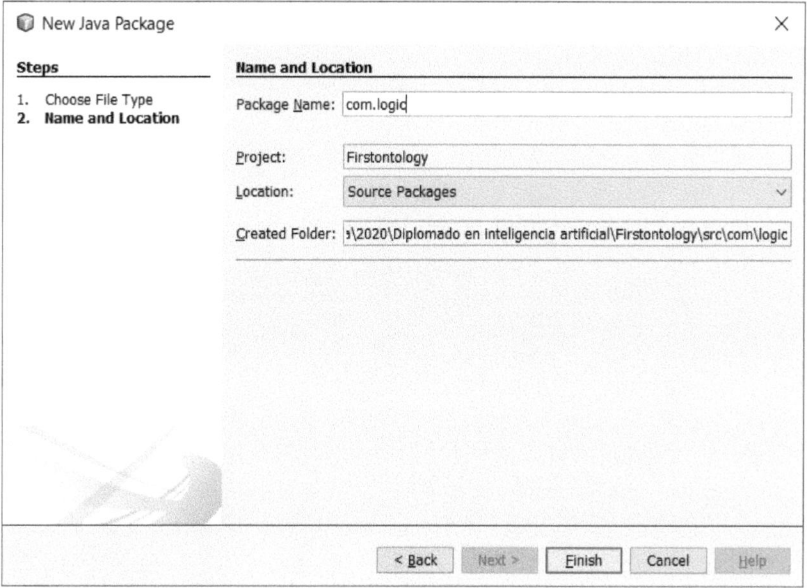

Figure 9. Package name

8. Locate the com.logic package and right click on New -> Java Class, see figure 10.

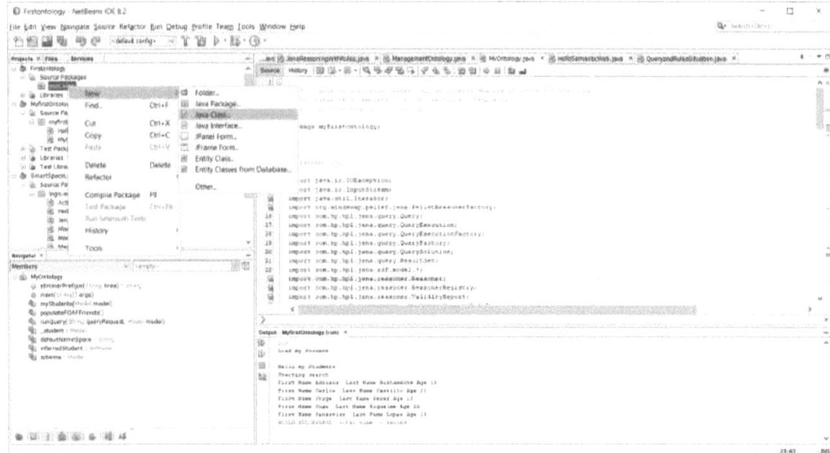

Figure 10. Creating a new class

9. In Class Name: type Searchontology, click Finish, see figure 11.

Figure 11. Class name.

10. Then copy and paste the following code under the Package com.logic header, as shown in Figure 12.

import java.io.IOException;
import java.io.InputStream;

```java
import java.util.Iterator;
import org.mindswap.pellet.jena.PelletReasonerFactory;
import com.hp.hpl.jena.query.Query;
import com.hp.hpl.jena.query.QueryExecution;
import com.hp.hpl.jena.query.QueryExecutionFactory;
import com.hp.hpl.jena.query.QueryFactory;
import com.hp.hpl.jena.query.QuerySolution;
import com.hp.hpl.jena.query.ResultSet;
import com.hp.hpl.jena.rdf.model.*;
import com.hp.hpl.jena.reasoner.Reasoner;
import com.hp.hpl.jena.reasoner.ReasonerRegistry;
import com.hp.hpl.jena.reasoner.ValidityReport;
import com.hp.hpl.jena.reasoner.rulesys.GenericRuleReasoner;
import com.hp.hpl.jena.reasoner.rulesys.Rule;
import com.hp.hpl.jena.util.FileManager;
```

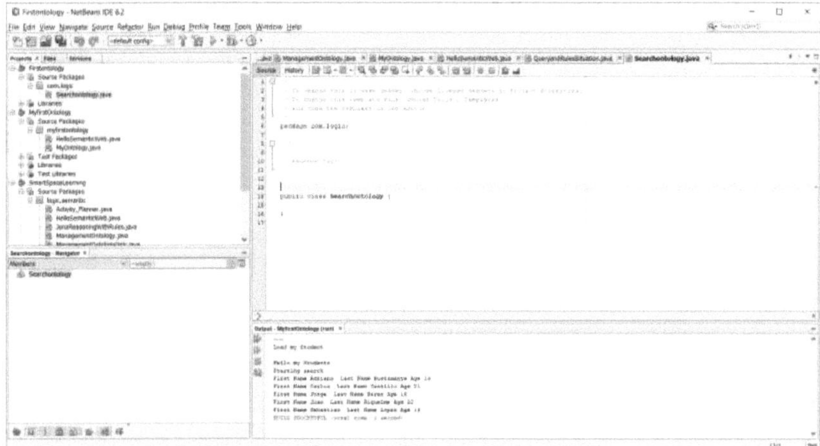

Figure 12. Skeleton of the class

11. Once you paste the code, you will see a list of errors with the libraries. These Apache Jena libraries are used to interact with ontologies. To correct these library errors. The errors are highlighted in figure 13.

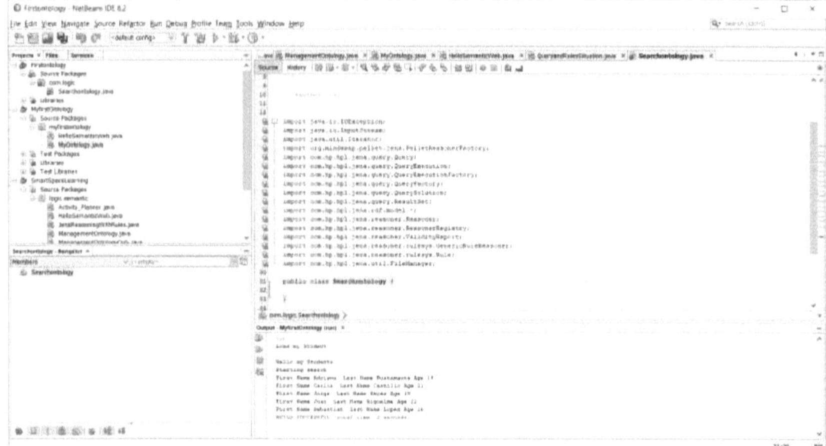

Figure 13. Error in libraries.

12.Next, to solve the problem with the libraries, right-click on the Firstontology project in the Properties option, see figure 14.

Figure 14. Definition of properties to assign libraries

13.Go to the Libraries section, then click on add JAR/Folder. See figure 15.

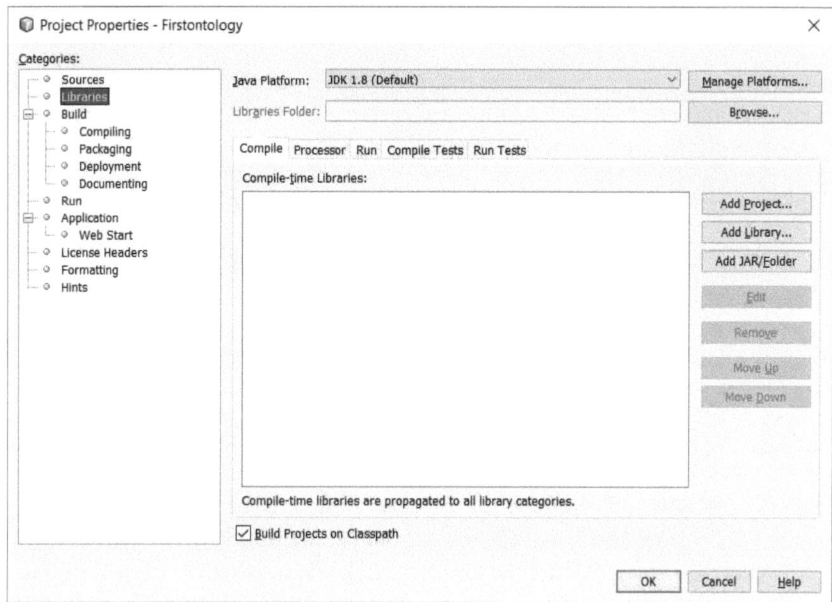

Figure 15. Library selection

14. Next locate the lib folder that you initially downloaded, double click on it and select all the libraries as shown in figures 16 and 17, then click Open.

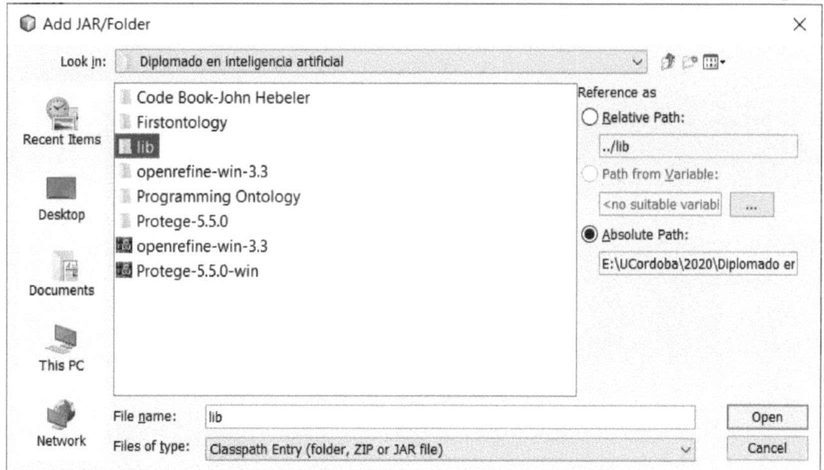

Figure 16. Identification of the folder containing the libraries.

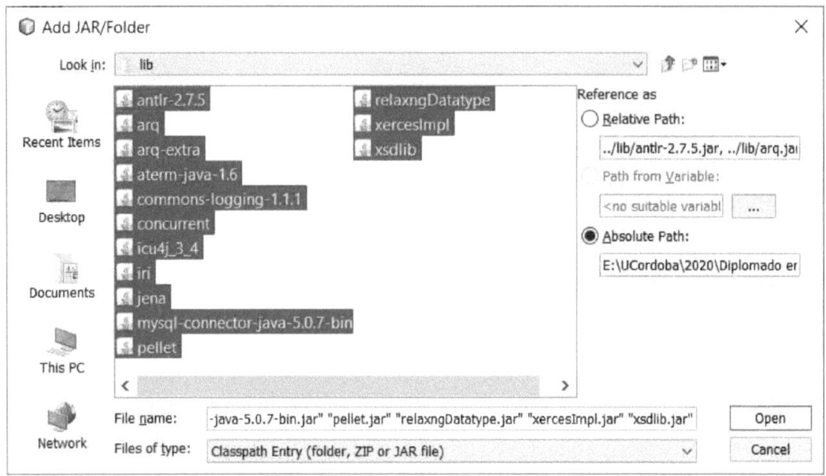

Figure 17. Selection of libraries.

15. After you have selected the libraries click OK, this will resolve the library errors. See figure 18.

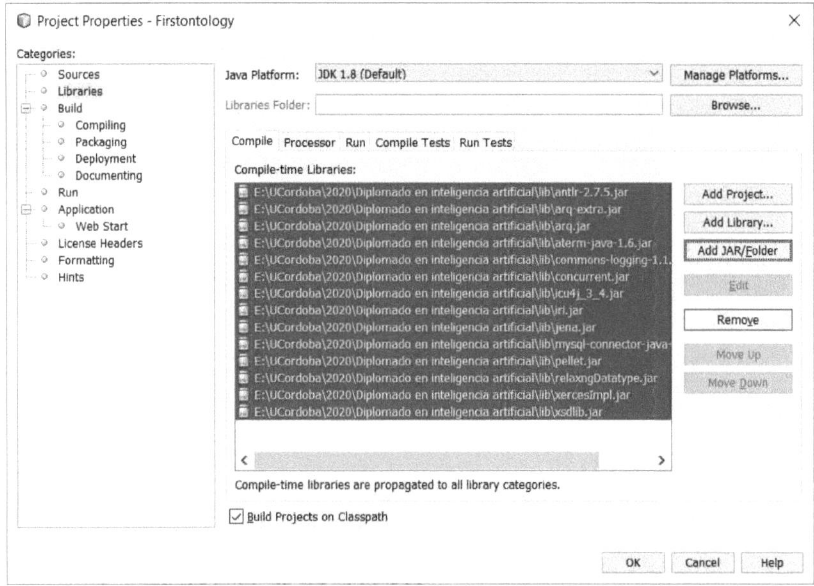

Figure 18. Adding libraries.

16. Then right-click on the Firstontology project. Click on New -> Java Folder. See figure 19.

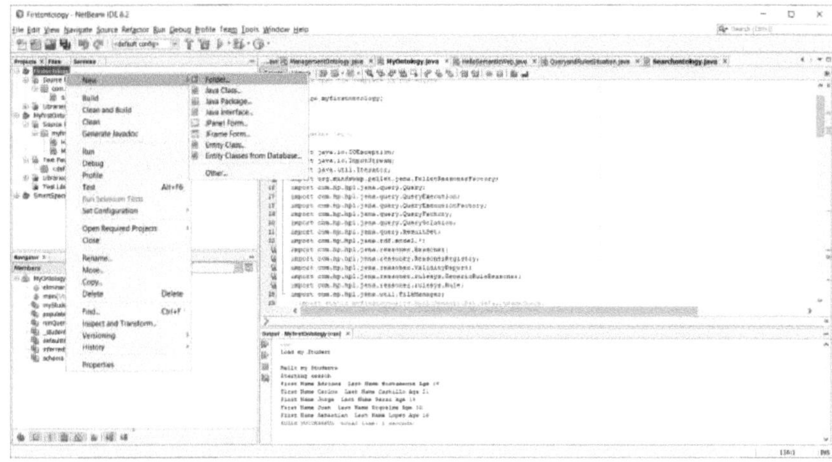

Figure 19. Folder creation for the project.

17.In Folder Name Name: type Ontologies, then click Finish. See figure 20.

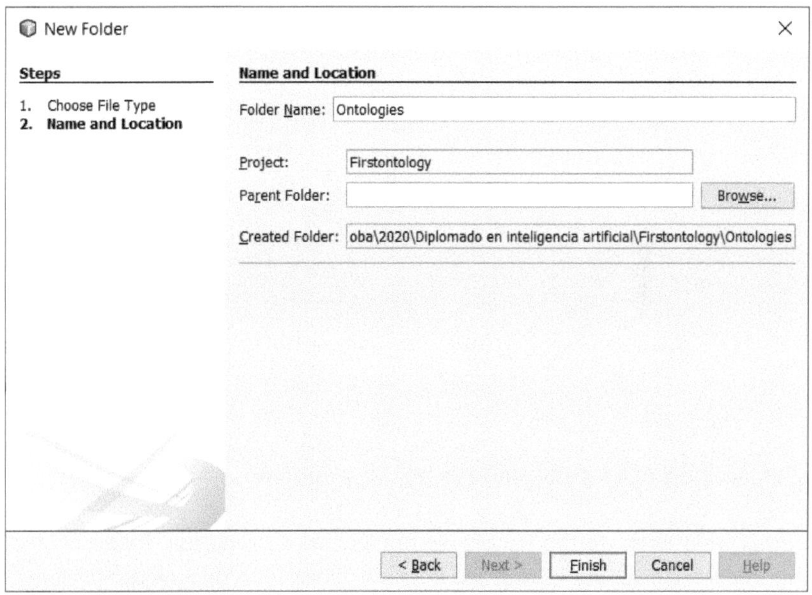

Figure 20. Project name

18.Next, find the path where you saved the project, see figure 21.

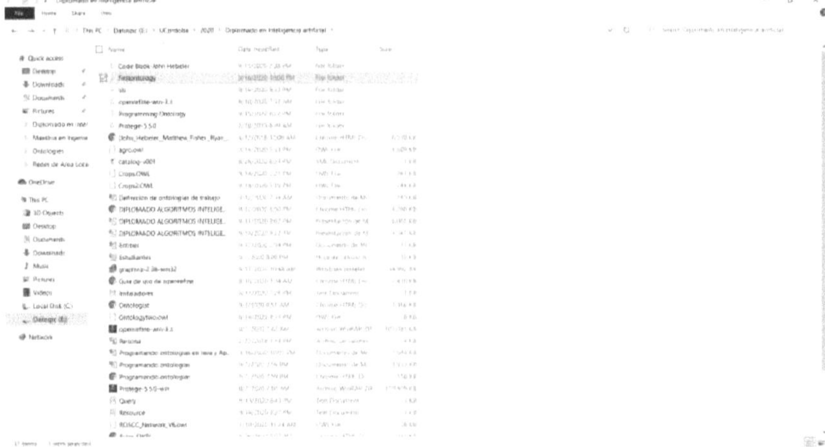

Figure 21. Location of the project

19. Double click on the Firstontology folder. See figure 22.

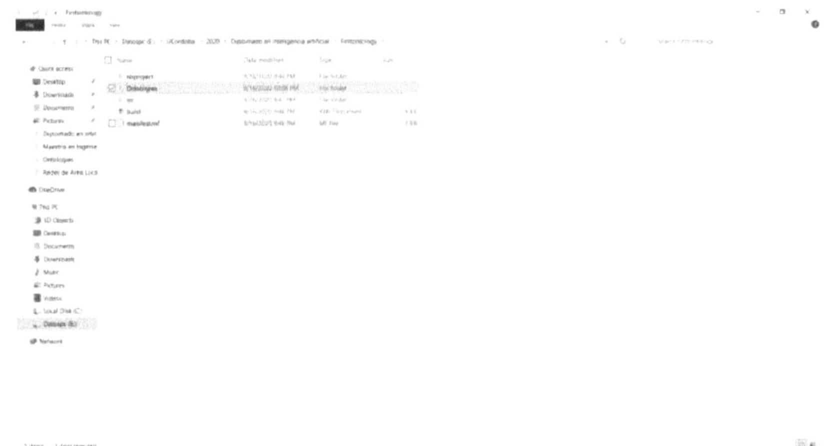

Figure 22. Folder where the ontology will be uploaded

20. Double click on the Ontologies folder, once inside this folder copy the SampleUniversity4.OWL file that you downloaded from the resource at the beginning of this practice. See figure 23.

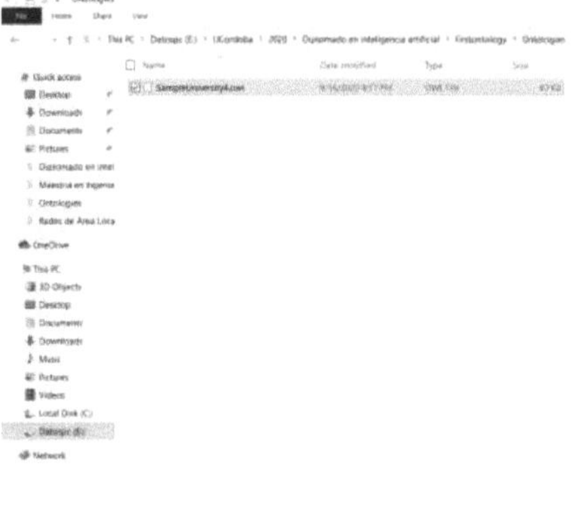

Figure 23. Folder containing the ontology

21. then select the code below and copy and paste it into the section
public class Searchontology {

```java
static             String             defaultNameSpace             =
"http://www.semanticweb.org/jegjo/ontologies/Myontology1#";

       Model _student = null;
       Model schema = null;
       InfModel inferredStudent = null;

       public static void main(String[] args) throws IOException {

               Searchontology myontology = new Searchontology();

               //Load my Students
               System.out.println("Load my Student");
               myontology.populateFOAFFriends();

               // List my student
               System.out.println("Hello my Students");
               myontology.myStudents(myontology._student);
```

```java
        }
    private void populateFOAFFriends(){
            _student = ModelFactory.createOntologyModel();
            InputStream                inFoafInstance                =
FileManager.get().open("Ontologies/SampleUniversity4.owl");
            _student.read(inFoafInstance,defaultNameSpace);
            //inFoafInstance.close();


        }
private void myStudents(Model model){
            //listing students
            runQuery("SELECT  ?  first_name  ?  last_name  ?  age  ?
name_group\n" ?
        WHERE { "WHERE" +
"Student ROSCC:First_Name ? first_name. \n" +
"Student ROSCC:is_Enrolled ROSCC:Grp0001.\n" +
" ?Student ROSCC:Last_Name ? last_name.\n" +
"Student ROSCC:Age ?age ?age.} \n" +
"          Orderby ? first_name ", model); //add the query string


        }
private void runQuery(String queryRequest, Model model){

            StringBuffer queryStr = new StringBuffer();
            // Establish Prefixes
            //Set default Name space first
            queryStr.append("PREFIX
ROSCC:<http://www.semanticweb.org/jegjo/ontologies/Myontology1#>");
 queryStr.append("PREFIX owl: <http://www.w3.org/2002/07/owl#>) ;
 queryStr.append("PREFIX rdf" + ": <" + "http://www.w3.org/1999/02/22-rdf-
syntax-ns#" + "> ");
 queryStr.append("PREFIX  rdfs" + ": <" + "http://www.w3.org/2000/01/rdf-
schema#" + "> ");


            queryStr.append("PREFIX      foaf"    +      ": <"     +
"http://xmlns.com/foaf/0.1/" + "> ");
```

```java
            //Now add query

            queryStr.append(queryRequest);
            Query query = QueryFactory.create(queryStr.toString());
            QueryExecution  qexec  =  QueryExecutionFactory.create(query,
model);
            try {
            ResultSet response = qexec.execSelect();
        System.out.println("Starting search");
            while( response.hasNext()){

                    QuerySolution soln = response.nextSolution();
                    RDFNode firstname = soln.get("? first_name");
                    RDFNode lastname = soln.get("? last_name");
 RDFNode age = soln.get("?age");


 if( (firstname != null) && (lastname != null) && (age != null)){
                        System.out.println(     "First     Name     "     +
firstname.toString() +" "+ " Last  Name " + lastname.toString()+" Age " +
age.toString());
                    }
                    else
                        System.out.println("No student found!");
                    }
            } finally { qexec.close();}
            }

public String deletePrefixes (String line){

line=line.replace("http://www.semanticweb.org/jegjo/ontologies/Myontology1#
", "");


    return line;
    }
```

22. Then right click on the Searchontology file, click on Run File. See figure
    24.

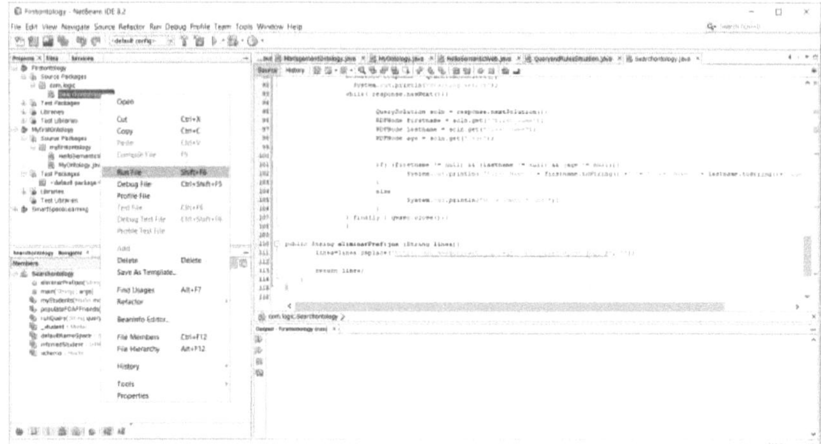

Figure 24. Execution of the class.

23.Finally, at the bottom of the screen you will see the results of the query. See figure 25.

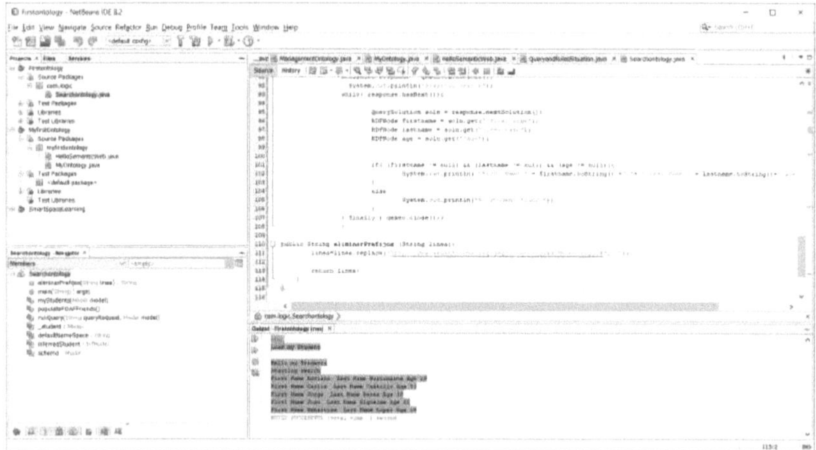

Figure 25. Results of the consultation

Explanation of the Code

Figure 26 shows the relationships between the different classes.

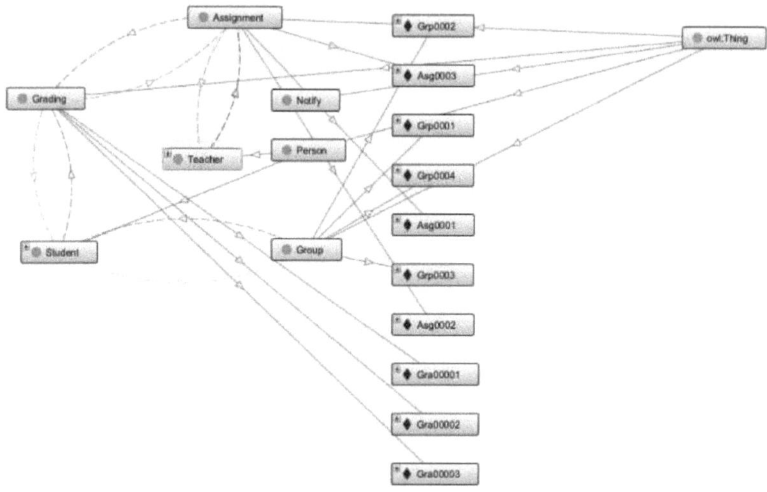

Figure 26. Representation of ontology classes, relations and instances.

In the case of the project in question, the following query will be executed in Sparql

```
PREFIX owl: <http://www.w3.org/2002/07/owl#>
 PREFIX rdf: <http://www.w3.org/1999/02/22-rdf-syntax-ns#>
            PREFIX rdfs: <http://www.w3.org/2000/01/rdf-schema#>
            PREFIX                                          ROSCC:
<http://www.semanticweb.org/jegjo/ontologies/Myontology1#>
 SELECT ? first_name ? last_name ? last_name ? age ? name_group

            WHERE {
Student ROSCC:First_Name ? first_name.
Student ROSCC:is_Enrrolled ROSCC:Grp0001.
Student ROSCC:Last_Name ? last_name.
 ?Student ROSCC:Age ?age.
            }
    Orderby ? first_name
```

In Protegé the result will be the one highlighted in blue in figure 27.

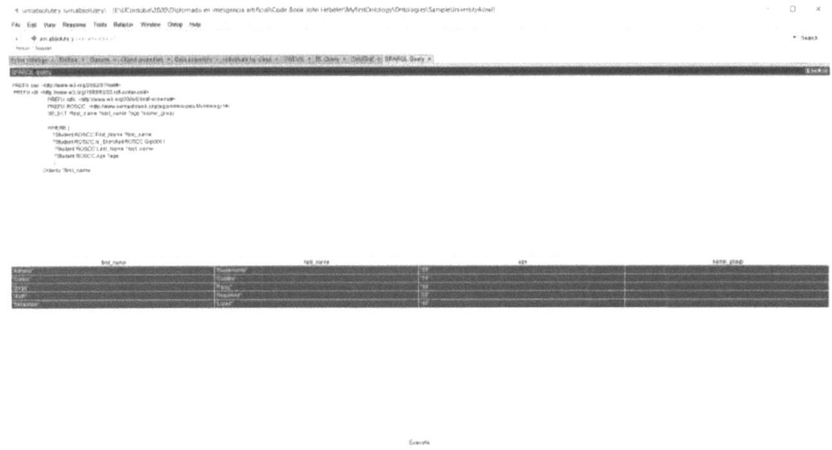

Figure 27. Result of a SparQL query in Protegé.

For the case of the Netbeans project. The implementation is given as follows: The namespace is explained in Figure 28.

Figure 28. Explanation of namespace

```
        Model _student = null;
        Model schema = null;
```

```
        InfModel inferredStudent = null;
```

The _student and schema of type Model are defined to load the model extracted from the query. inferredStudent allows to run the inference from the reasoner.

```
Searchontology myontology = new Searchontology();
```

Searchontology class is installed in myontology
This section allows the ontology file to be loaded using the populateFOAFFriends() method.

```
//Load my Students
        System.out.println("Load my Student");
        myontology.populateFOAFFriends();
```

The invocation of the populateFOAFFriends() method, allows to extract the ontology from the OWL file, SampleUniversity4.owl

```
private void populateFOAFFriends(){
        _student = ModelFactory.createOntologyModel();
        InputStream inFoafInstance =
FileManager.get().open("Ontologies/SampleUniversity4.owl");
        _student.read(inFoafInstance,defaultNameSpace);
        //inFoafInstance.close();

    }
```

The myStudents method, allows you to define the query that will display the students' information.

```
private void myStudents(Model model model){
        //listing students
        runQuery("SELECT  ?  first_name  ?  last_name  ?  age  ?
name_group\n" ?
    WHERE { "WHERE" +
"Student ROSCC:First_Name ? first_name. \n" +
"Student ROSCC:is_Enrrolled ROSCC:Grp0001.\n" +
" ?Student ROSCC:Last_Name ? last_name.\n" +
"Student ROSCC:Age ?age ?age.} \n" +
```

```
"              Orderby ? first_name ", model); //add the query string


      }
```

The runQuery method allows adding the URL prefixes of the ontologies to be used, then the myStudents query model is loaded.

```
private void runQuery(String queryRequest, Model model){


          StringBuffer queryStr = new StringBuffer();
          // Establish Prefixes
          //Set default Name space first
          queryStr.append("PREFIX
ROSCC:<http://www.semanticweb.org/jegjo/ontologies/Myontology1#>");
 queryStr.append("PREFIX owl: <http://www.w3.org/2002/07/owl#>) ;
 queryStr.append("PREFIX rdf" + ": <" + "http://www.w3.org/1999/02/22-rdf-
syntax-ns#" + "> ");
 queryStr.append("PREFIX rdfs" + ": <" + "http://www.w3.org/2000/01/rdf-
schema#" + "> ");


          queryStr.append("PREFIX      foaf"    +      ":    <"    +
"http://xmlns.com/foaf/0.1/" + "> ");


          //Now add query

          queryStr.append(queryRequest);
          Query query = QueryFactory.create(queryStr.toString());
          QueryExecution  qexec  =  QueryExecutionFactory.create(query,
model);
          try {
          ResultSet response = qexec.execSelect();
      System.out.println("Starting search");
          while( response.hasNext()){

              QuerySolution soln = response.nextSolution();
              RDFNode firstname = soln.get("? first_name");
              RDFNode lastname = soln.get("? last_name");
 RDFNode age = soln.get("?age");
```

```
if( (firstname != null) && (lastname != null) && (age != null)){
                System.out.println(    "First    Name    "    +
firstname.toString() +" "+ " Last Name " + lastname.toString()+" Age " +
age.toString());
                }
            else
                System.out.println("No student found!");
            }
        } finally { qexec.close();}
        }
```

```
PREFIX owl: <http://www.w3.org/2002/07/owl#>
PREFIX rdf: <http://www.w3.org/1999/02/22-rdf-syntax-ns#>
                PREFIX    rdfs:    <http://www.w3.org/2000/01/rdf-
schema#>
                PREFIX                        ROSCC:
<http://www.semanticweb.org/jegjo/ontologies/Myontology1#>
SELECT ? first_name ? last_name ?age

                WHERE {
Student ROSCC:First_Name ? first_name.
Student ROSCC:is_Enrrolled ROSCC:Grp0001.
Student ROSCC:Last_Name ? last_name.
 ?Student ROSCC:Age ?age.
Filter(?age >'16')
}
Orderby ? first_name
```

4.2. ONTOLOGY MANAGEMENT WITH RESTFUL WEB SERVICE WITH JAVA

Requirements

Netbeans 12.1

https://downloads.apache.org/netbeans/netbeans/12.1

Important

We are going to use Payara Server as our server. Since it comes with the default Javax.ws.rs library which is required.

In case that at the moment of running the server an error is generated by the use of JDK 13 that comes by default with this version of NetBeans 12.1, we would have to install JDK version 8U111 (1.8).

https://www.oracle.com/technetwork/es/java/javase/downloads/jdk-netbeans-jsp-3413139-esa.html

We go to the New Project icon and click on

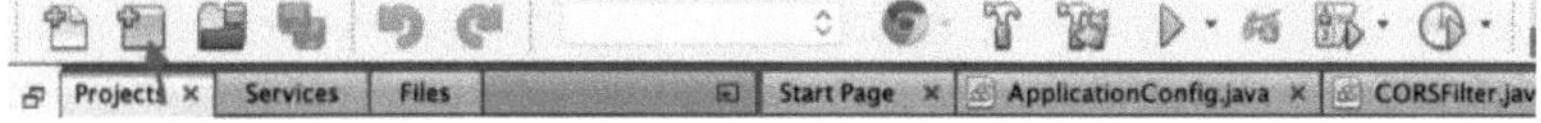

Select Java with Ant, Java Web and finally Web Application.

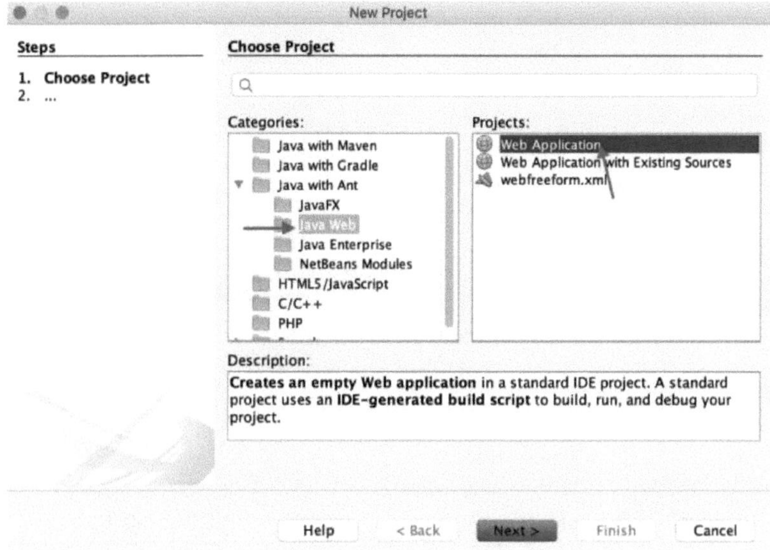

Type in the name of the project and press Next

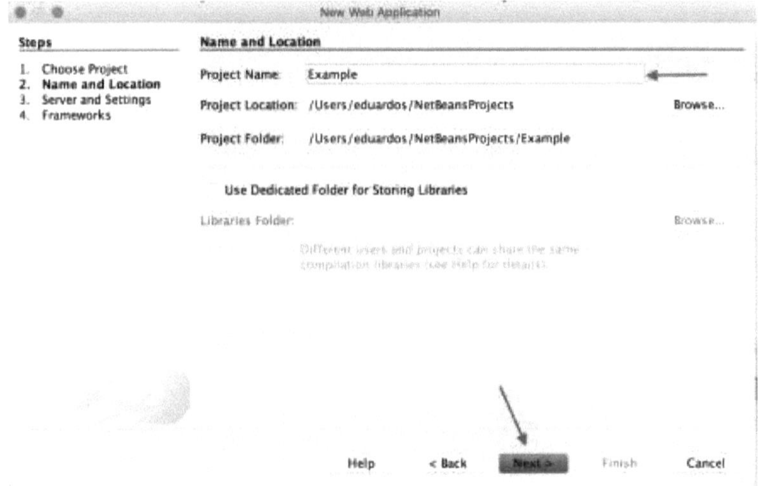

Select **Payara Server** and click Finish

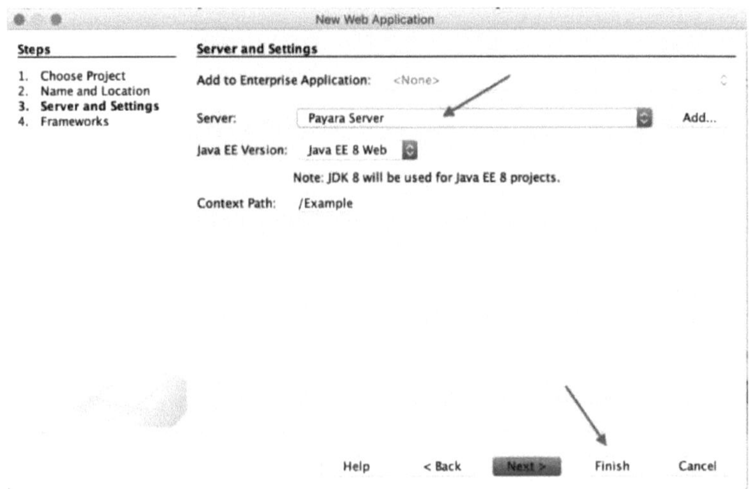

Once the project is created, right click, New, and select the **RESTful Web Services from Patterns** option.

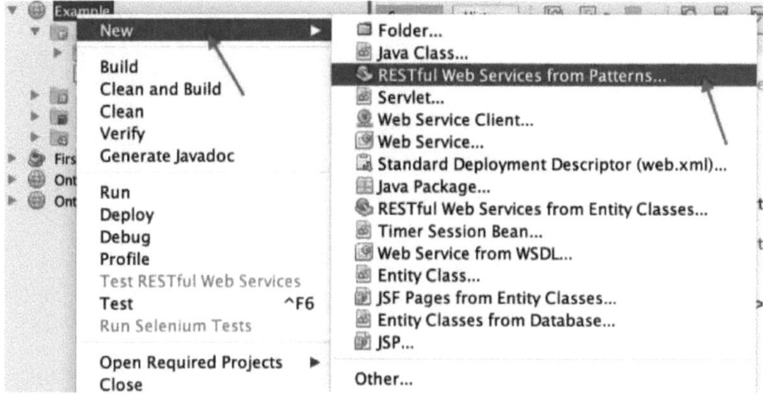

Select the first option and press Next

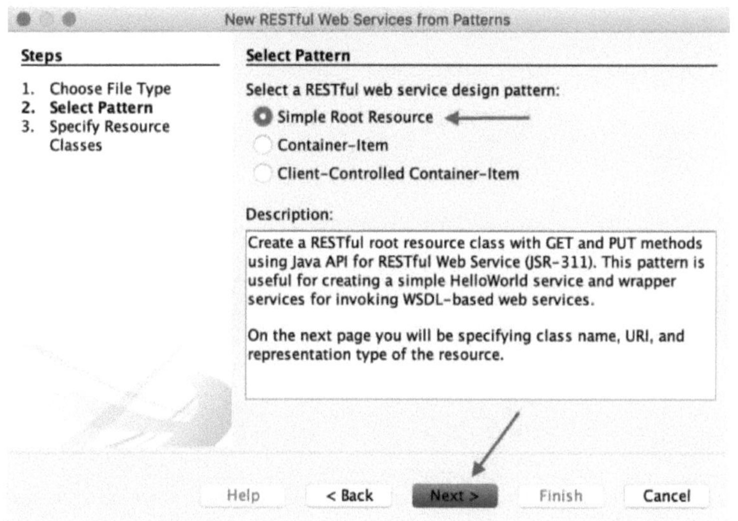

The project name should appear by default. We write a name for the package, by convention, **API**.

Leave the rest of the configuration as default and press Finish.

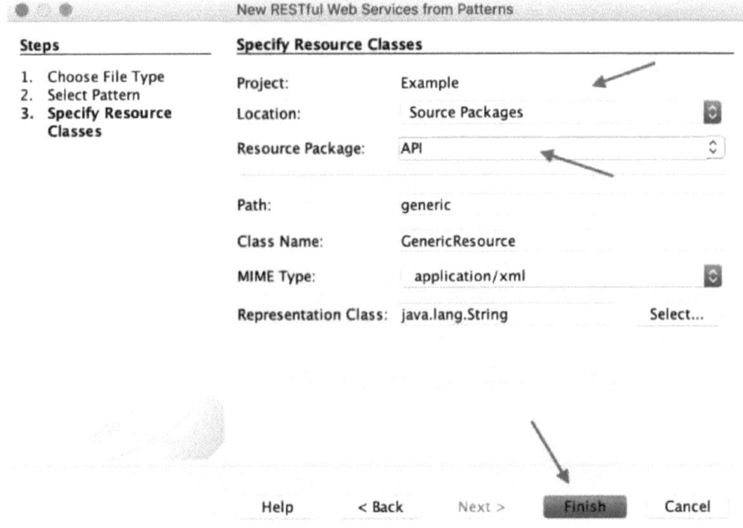

This is the structure that is created for us.

The **GenericResources** file contains two endpoints that are mirrored inside the **RESTful Web Services** folder. If we delete either of them, they will also be deleted from the other location.

Now we could run the server and use one of these two endpoints. But first we will modify this file to return the JSON of the OWL queries we make.

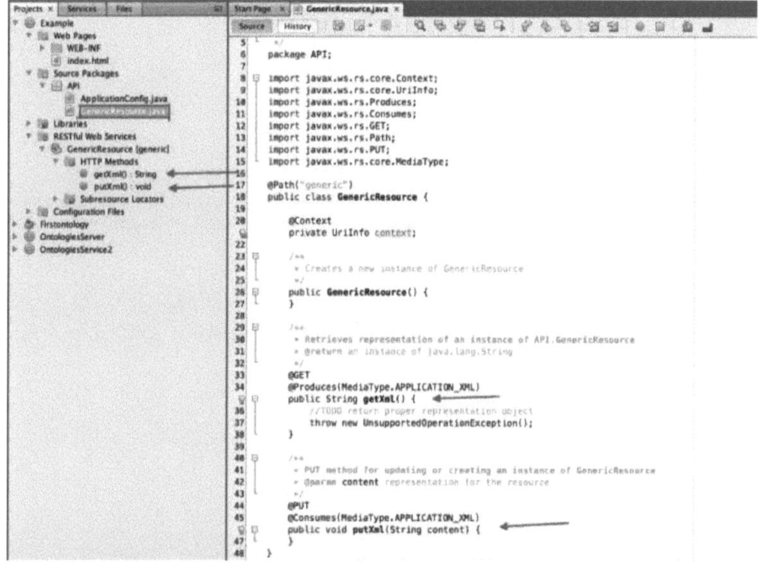

MODIFICATION OF FILES

Taking into account the following image of how our project will look like, we must add the **CORSFilter.java** files for the CORS management and the **SampleUniversity4.owl** file which contains the classes, properties and instances to perform the queries.

In addition, modify the **GenericResources.java** file to add the code that receives our GET request and executes the query.

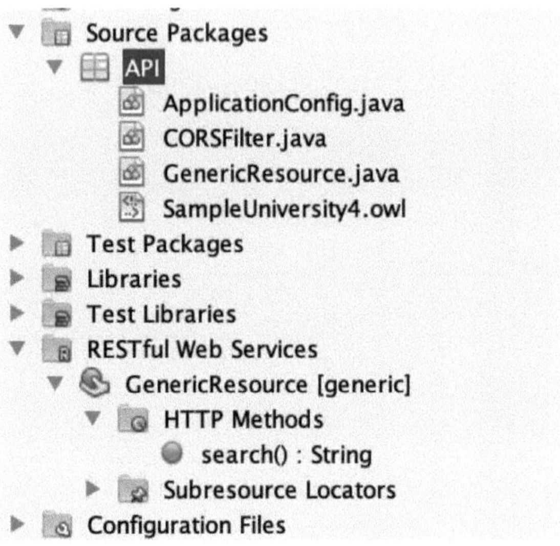

CORSFilter.java FILE CODE

This file is in charge of configuring the CORS policies, so that our server does not reject requests from any client.

```java
import javax.ws.rs. container.ContainerRequestContext;

import javax.ws.rs. container.ContainerResponseContext;

import javax.ws.rs. container.ContainerResponseFilter;

import javax.ws.rs.ext.Provider;

@Provider

public class CORSFilter implements ContainerResponseFilter {

@Override

public void filter(final ContainerRequestContext requestContext, final
ContainerResponseContext cres) throws IOException {

cres.getHeaders().add("Access-Control-Allow-Origin", "*");

cres.getHeaders().add("Access-Control-Allow-Headers", "origin, content-
type, accept, authorization");

cres.getHeaders().add("Access-Control-Allow-Credentials", "true");

cres.getHeaders().add("Access-Control-Allow-Methods", "GET, POST,
PUT, DELETE, OPTIONS, HEAD");

cres.getHeaders().add("Access-Control-Max-Age", "1209600");

}

}
```

FILE CODE SampleUniversity4.owl

The code of this file will be sent with this documentation. It contains all the Classes, instances, relations and properties needed to make the queries.

GenericResources.java FILE CODE

```java
import javax.ws.rs.core.Context;

import javax.ws.rs.core.UriInfo;

import javax.ws.rs.Produces;

import javax.ws.rs.GET;

import javax.ws.rs.Path;

import javax.ws.rs.core.MediaType;

import javax.ws.rs.QueryParam;


import com.hp.hpl.jena.query.Query;

import com.hp.hpl.jena.query.QueryExecution;

import com.hp.hpl.jena.query.QueryExecutionFactory;

import com.hp.hpl.jena.query.QueryFactory;

import com.hp.hpl.jena.query.QuerySolution;

import com.hp.hpl.jena.query.ResultSet;

import com.hp.hpl.jena.rdf.model.*;

import com.hp.hpl.jena.util.FileManager;

import java.io.InputStream;

import javax.ws.rs.DefaultValue;
```

```java
/**

REST  Web Service

*

*@author eduardos */ @Path("generic")

public class GenericResource {

static String defaultNameSpace =
"http://www.semanticweb.org/jegjo/ontologies/Myontology1#"; Model _student = null;

Model schema = null;

InfModel inferredStudent = null;



@Context
private UriInfo context;

/**

      *Creates a new instance of GenericResource */

public GenericResource() {

}

/**

      *Retrieves representation of an instance of API.GenericResource

      *@return an instance of java.lang.String

*/

@GET

@Produces(MediaType.APPLICATION_JSON)
```

```java
public String search(

@DefaultValue("1") @QueryParam("option") String option,

@DefaultValue("Grp0001") @QueryParam("group") String group,

@DefaultValue("") @QueryParam("comparative") String comparative,

@DefaultValue("") @QueryParam("assignment") String assignment,

@DefaultValue("") @QueryParam("gender") String gender,

@DefaultValue("") @QueryParam("age") String age,

@DefaultValue("") @QueryParam("grade") String grade

) {

GenericResource myontology = new GenericResource();

myontology.populateFOAFFriends();


String json = myontology.myStudents(myontology._student, option, age, comparative, group,
assignment, grade, gender); return json;

}


private void populateFOAFFriends(){

_student = ModelFactory.createOntologyModel();

InputStream inFoafInstance =

FileManager.get().open("/Users/eduardos/NetBeansProjects/OntologiesService2/src/java/API/
SampleUniversity4.owl");

_student.read(inFoafInstance,defaultNameSpace);

}

private String myStudents(Model model, String option, String age, String
```

```java
comparativeExpression, String group, String assignment, String grade, String gender){

String query = "";

switch (option) {

case "1": {

query = "SELECT ? first_name ? last_name ? age ? name_group\n" ?

"       WHERE {" +

"          ?Student ROSCC:First_Name ? first_name. \n" +

"          ?Student ROSCC:is_Enrrolled ROSCC:" + group + ".\n" +

"          ?Student ROSCC:Last_Name ? last_name.name.\n" +

"          ?Student ROSCC:Age ?age.} \n" +

"          Orderby ? first_name";

break;

}

case "2": {

query = "SELECT ? first_name ? last_name ? age" ?

"       WHERE {" +

"          ?Student ROSCC:First_Name ? first_name. \n" +

"          ?Student ROSCC:is_Enrrolled ROSCC:" + group + ". \n" +

"          ?Student ROSCC:Last_Name ? last_name. \n" +

"          ?Student ROSCC:Age ?age. Filter(?age "+ comparativeExpression + """ + age + "") }
\n" +

"          Orderby ? first_name";

break;
```

```java
}

case "3": {

query = "SELECT ? first_name ? last_name ? age" ?

"       WHERE {" +

"         ?Teacher ROSCC:First_Name ? first_name. \n" +

"         ?Teacher ROSCC:is_Imparted ROSCC:" + assignment + ". \n" +

"         ?Teacher ROSCC:Last_Name ? last_name. \n" +

"         ?Teacher ROSCC:Age ?age.} \n" +

"         Orderby ? first_name";

break;

}

case "4": {

query = "SELECT ? first_name ? last_name ? age" ?

"       WHERE {" +

"         ?Student ROSCC:First_Name ? first_name. \n" +

"         ?Grading ROSCC:is_A_Student ?Student. \n" +

"         ?Student ROSCC:Age ?age. \n" +

"         ?Student ROSCC:Last_Name ? last_name.name.\n" +

"         ?Grading ROSCC:Finish_Grade ? finish_grade. Filter(? finish_grade " +
comparativeExpression + "'" + grade + "') } \n" +

"         Orderby ? first_name";

break;

}
```

```java
case "5": {

query = "SELECT ? first_name ? last_name ? age" ?

"        WHERE {" +

"        ?Teacher ROSCC:First_Name ? first_name. \n" +

"        ?Teacher ROSCC:is_Imparted ?assignment. \n" +

"        ?Teacher ROSCC:Last_Name ? last_name. \n" +

"        ?Teacher ROSCC:Age ?age. \n" +

"        ?Teacher ROSCC:Gender ?gender. Filter(?gender = '" + gender + "') } \n" +

"        Orderby ? first_name";

break;

}

default: return "";

}

//listing students

return runQuery(query, model); //add the query string

}


private String runQuery(String queryRequest, Model model){

StringBuffer queryStr = new StringBuffer();

// Establish Prefixes

//Set default Name space first

queryStr.append("PREFIX
```

```java
ROSCC:<http://www.semanticweb.org/jegjo/ontologies/Myontology1#>");
queryStr.append("PREFIX owl: <http://www.w3.org/2002/07/owl#>") ;
queryStr.append("PREFIX rdf" + ": <" + "http://www.w3.org/1999/02/22-rdfsyntax-ns#" + ">
"); queryStr.append("PREFIX rdfs" + ": <" + "http://www.w3.org/2000/01/rdfschema#" + ">
"); queryStr.append("PREFIX foaf" + ": <" + "http://xmlns.com/foaf/0.1/" + ">");

//Now add query


queryStr.append(queryRequest);

Query query = QueryFactory.create(queryStr.toString());

QueryExecution qexec = QueryExecutionFactory.create(query, model);


String json = "";


try {

ResultSet response = qexec.execSelect();

System.out.println("Starting search");


while(response.hasNext()){


QuerySolution soln = response.nextSolution();

RDFNode firstname = soln.get("? first_name");

RDFNode lastname = soln.get("? last_name");

RDFNode age = soln.get("?age");


if( (firstname != null) && (lastname != null) && (age != null)){

json += "{"name":\""+ firstname.toString() +"\"," +

""last_name":\""+ lastname.toString() +"\"," +

"age "age "+ age.toString() +"age"}";
```

```java
if (response.hasNext())) json += ",";

} else {

System.out.println("No data found!");

}

}

} finally { qexec.close();

}

return "[" + json + "]";

}

}
```

This file contains a GET endpoint which is called **search**. Inside it, the **QueryParameters** that are sent from the client application are obtained.

<h1 style="text-align:center">IMPORTANT</h1>

In the **populateFOAFFriends()** method, the location of the **SampleUniversity4.owl** file must be replaced by the location on your computer.

```java
}

private void populateFOAFFriends(){
    _student = ModelFactory.createOntologyModel();
    InputStream inFoafInstance = FileManager.get().open("/Users/eduardas/NetBeansProjects/OntologiesService2/src/java/API/SampleUniversity4.owl");
    _student.read(inFoafInstance,defaultNameSpace);
}
```

Otherwise, it will give an error when querying because it will not find the file.

With this, you have already implemented your RESTFul Web Service in Java. All we need is any client to consume it.

<h1 style="text-align:center">EXAMPLE OF CLIENT APPLICATION</h1>

This client consists of an HTML file in which we import styles from the Bootstrap CSS framework and make use of the AXIOS library to make the GET request to our server. In addition, we make use of a file called Index.js to obtain the HTML data and make the request.

IMPORTANT: Both files must be in the same folder.

<h1 style="text-align:center">INDEX.HTML FILE CODE</h1>

```html
<!DOCTYPE html>

<html lang="en">

<head>

<meta charset="UTF-8">

<meta name="viewport" content="width=device-width, initial-scale=1.0">

<link rel="stylesheet" href="https://stackpath.bootstrapcdn.com/bootstrap/5.0.0-alpha1/css/bootstrap.min.css" integrity="sha384-
```

r4NyP46KrjDleawBgD5tp8Y7UzmLA05oM1iAEQ17CSuDqnUK2+k9luXQOf
XJCJ4I" crossorigin="anonymous">

<title>Web Ontologies</title>.

</head>

<body style="background: #fafafa;">

<div class="container pt-4">

<div class="row">

<div class="col-4">

<div class="border bg-white rounded p-4">

<h4 class="mb-4">Menu</h4>

<div class="row">

<div class="col-6">

<h6> Option</h6>

<input id="option" type="text" class="form-control mb-3">

</div>

<div class="col-6">

<h6>Group</h6>.

<input id="group" type="text" class="form-control mb-3">

</div>

<div class="col-6">

<h6>Comparative sign</h6>.

<input id="comparative" type="text" class="form-control mb-3">

</div>

<div class="col-6">

<h6> Course</h6>

<input id="assignment" type="text" class="form-control mb-3">

</div>

<div class="col-6">

<h6> Gender</h6>.

<input id="gender" type="text" class="form-control mb-3">

</div>

<div class="col-6">

<h6> Age</h6>.

<input id="age" type="text" class="form-control mb-3">

</div>

<div class="col-12">

<h6>Note</h6>.

<input id="grade" type="text" class="form-control mb-4">

</div>

<div class="col-12">

<button class="btn btn-primary btn-block" onclick="send()"> Search</button> </div> </div>

</div>

</div>

<div class="col-8">

<div class="border bg-white rounded p-4 mb-4">

<h4 class="mb-4"> Consultations available</h4>.

<div class="row">

< div class="col-6">

<p>1. List students by group</p> 2.

</div>

<div class="col-6">

<p>2. List students by group and age</p> <p>3.

</div>

<div class="col-6">

<p>3. List teachers by subject</p> <p>3.

</div>

<div class="col-6">

<p>4. List students by grades</p> <p>5.

```html
</div>

<div class="col-6">

<p>5. List teachers by gender</p> <p>5.

</div>

</div>

</div>

<div class="border bg-white rounded p-4">

<h4 class="mb-4"> Result</h4>

<div id="result"></div>

</div>

</div>

</div>

</div>

<script src="_COPY16@1.16.0/dist/umd/popper.min.js" integrity="sha384-Q6E9RHvbIyZFJoft+2mJbHaEWldlvI9IOYy5n3zV9zzTtmI3UksdQRVvoxMfooAo" crossorigin="anonymous"></script>

<script src="https://stackpath.bootstrapcdn.com/bootstrap/5.0.0-alpha1/js/bootstrap.min.js" integrity="sha384-oesi62hOLfzrys4LxRF63OJCXdXDipiYWBnvTl9Y9/TRlw5xlKIEHpNyvvDShgf/" crossorigin="anonymous"></script>

<script src="https://cdn.jsdelivr.net/npm/axios/dist/axios.min.js"></script>
<script src="./index.js"></script>
```

```html
</body>

</html>
```

```javascript
const send = async () => {

const option = document.getElementById('option').value

const group = document.getElementById('group').value

const comparative = document.getElementById('comparative').value

const assignment = document.getElementById('assignment').value

const gender = document.getElementById('gender').value

const age = document.getElementById('age').value

const grade = document.getElementById('grade').value


const queryParams =

`?option=${option}&group=${group}&comparative=${comparative}&assignment=${assign
ment}&gender=${gender}&age=${age}&grade =${grade}`


try {

const { data } = await
axios.get(`http://localhost:8080/OntologiesService2/webresources/generic${queryParams}`)

const resultDiv = document.getElementById('result')

let stringHtml = '<div class="alert alert alert-primary" role="alert">No results</div>'


if (data.length > 0) {

const items = data.map(item =>

`<tr>

<td>${item.name}< /td>

<td>${item.last_name}</td>
```

```javascript
<td>${item.age} years</td>

</tr>``

).join('')

stringHtml =

`<table class="table">

< thead>

<tr>

< th scope="col"> Name</th>

< th scope="col"> Surnames</th>

<th scope="col"> Age</th>

</tr>

</thead>

< tbody>${items}</tbody>

</table>``

}


resultDiv.innerHTML = stringHtml

} catch (err) { console.log(err)

}

}
```

IMPORTANT

You must change the URL found in the **axios.get**() method to the one generated by your server.

```
try {
    const { data } = await axios.get(`http://localhost:8080/OntologiesService2/webresources/generic${queryParams}`)
    const resultDiv = document.getElementById('result')
    let stringHtml = '<div class="alert alert-primary" role="alert">Sin resultados</div>'
```

To generate that URL you must right click on your project and press the RUN option. Once it is running, right click on the **search() : String** method and press **Test Resource Uri**.

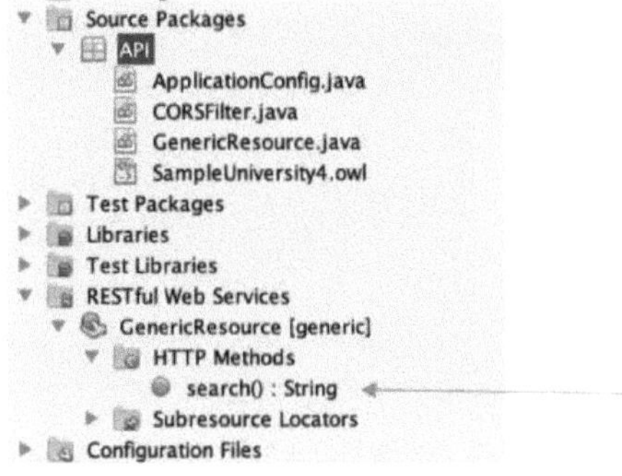

Once the above code has been implemented in their respective files, we can open **Index.html**

We will be shown a web page like the following one in which we could enter the values for each query and we will see the results of our **RESTFul Web Service**.

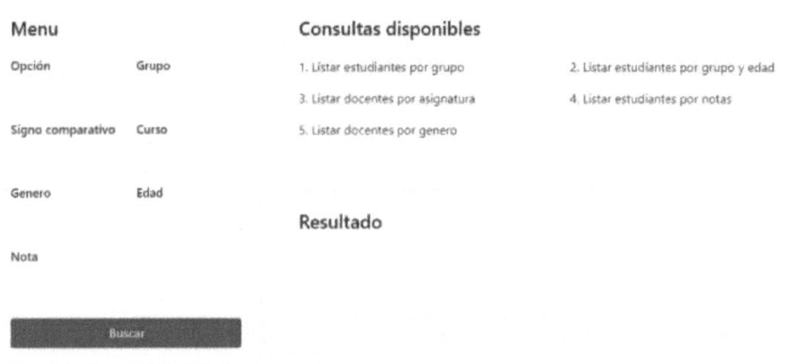

For example, if you want to execute query 1. You must enter in the option field the number 1 and in the group field, the group by which you want to filter. For example, Grp0001.

4.3. Creation of Web Service for Ontology Use

This guide shows the step-by-step in the creation of a web service to query ontologies, it will not show the step-by-step in the creation of the client web application that consumes this web service.
Netbeans Version 11.3
1. First create a new project by clicking on the new project button, then select "Ant -> Web Aplication".

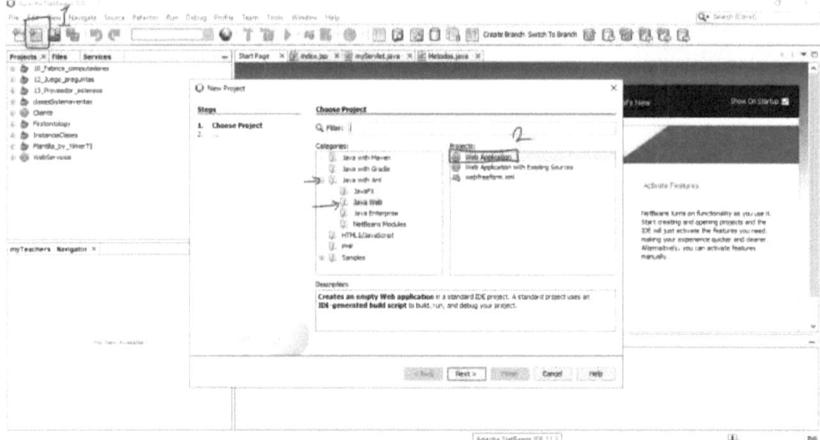

2. Then we name our project in this case "WebServices" and press next.

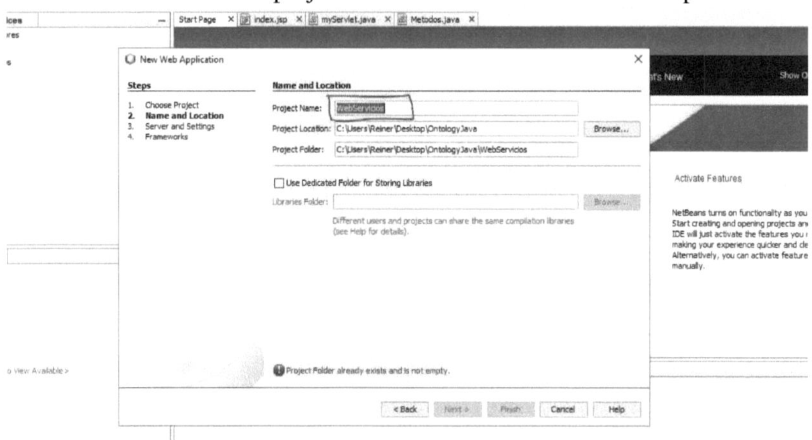

3. Choose the glassfish server and the latest Java EE version and press
   FINISH.

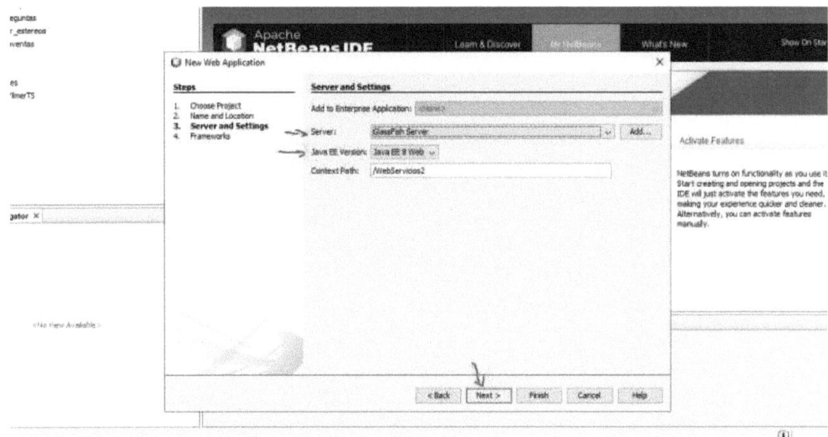

4. We will be left with something like this.

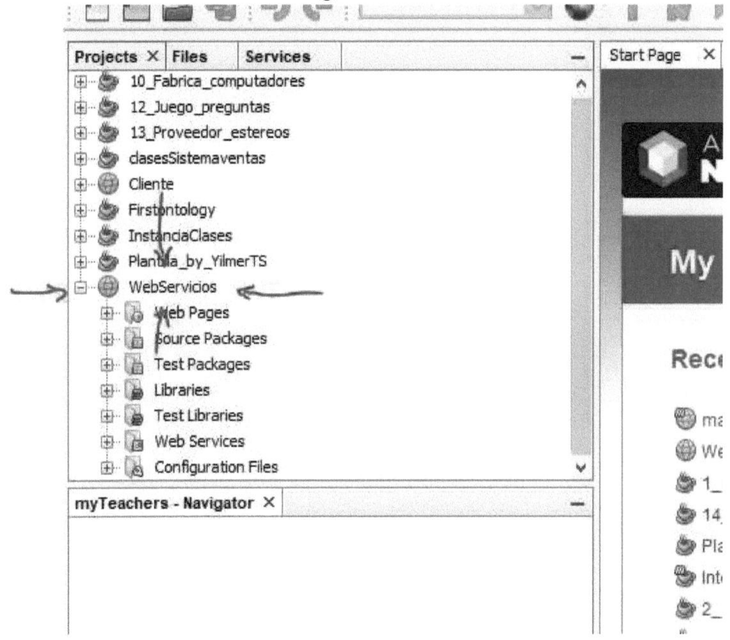

5. We right click on our project, then choose New -> WebService, we name
    it WebService and in package name we name it WS and press FINISH. As

shown below.

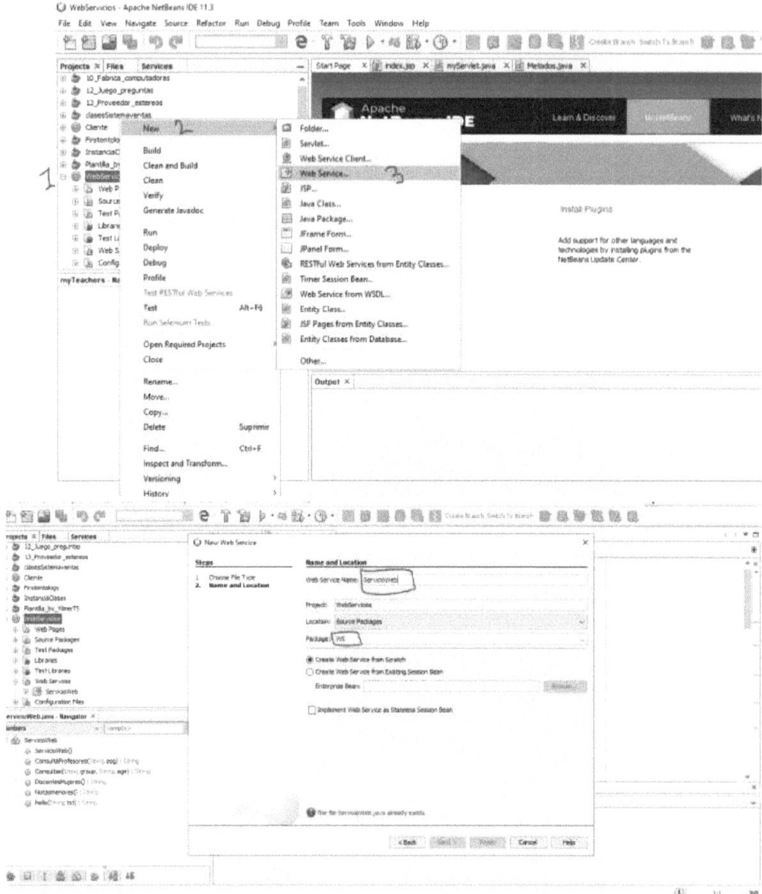

6. It will generate something like what we see in the following image, we
    can clearly see that we have created our Web Service but it only has a
    query called hello.

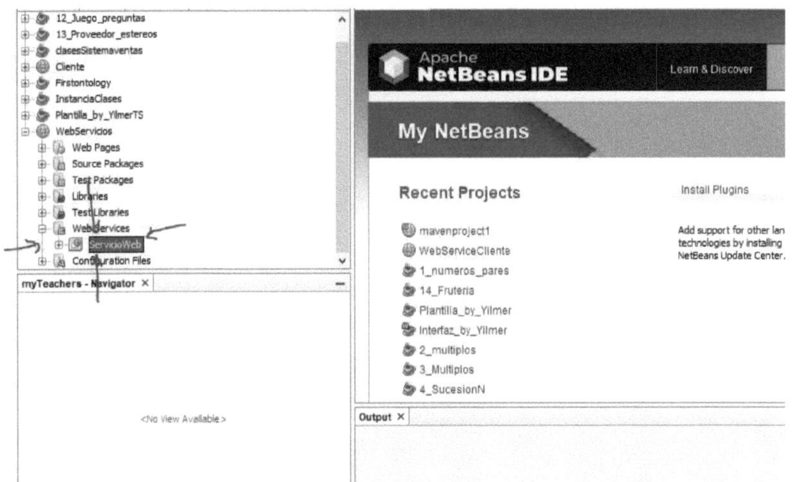

7. Now we will create a class called "Methods" in the package called WS that was automatically created when we created the WebService, to do so we right click on the WS package -> New - > Class Java

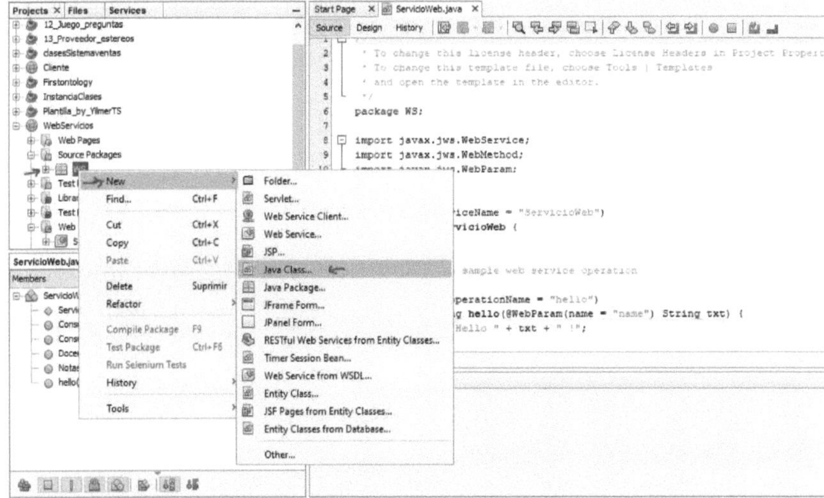

8. We name our Java class "Methods" and it is in this class where we will put all the code that will interact with our ontology.

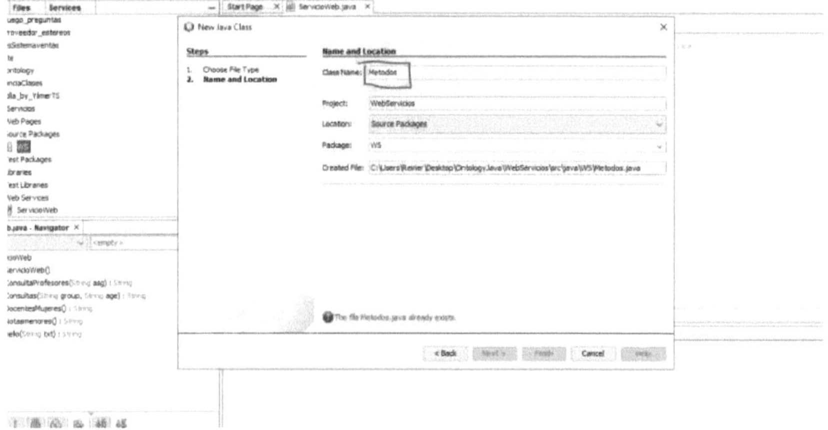

9. Now we will proceed to import the libraries that will be used by our web service by right clicking on the "Libraries" folder in our project and then "Add JAR/folder...".

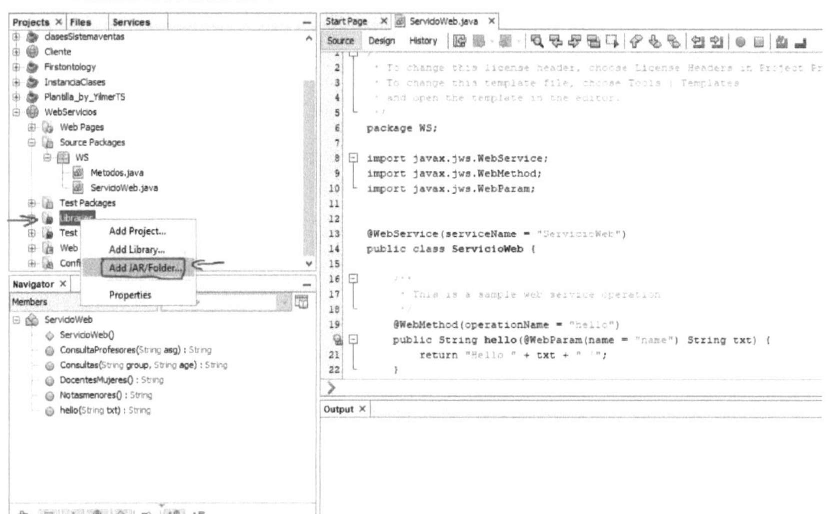

10. Browse to the location of the downloaded libraries on your computer, select all the libraries and press "Open".

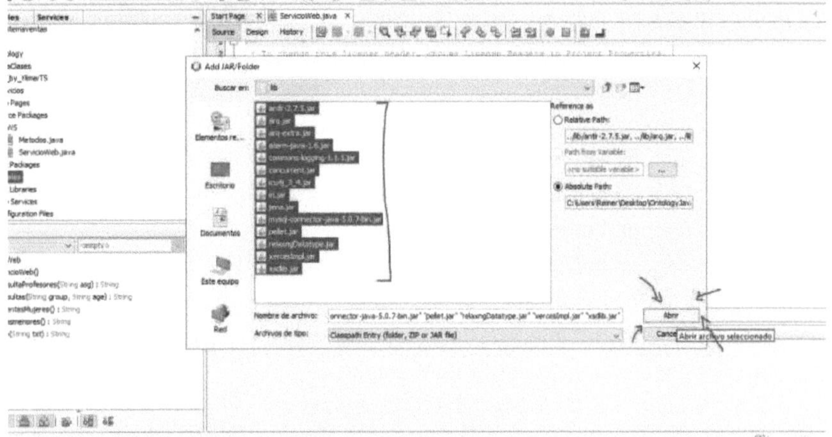

We should be left with something like this.

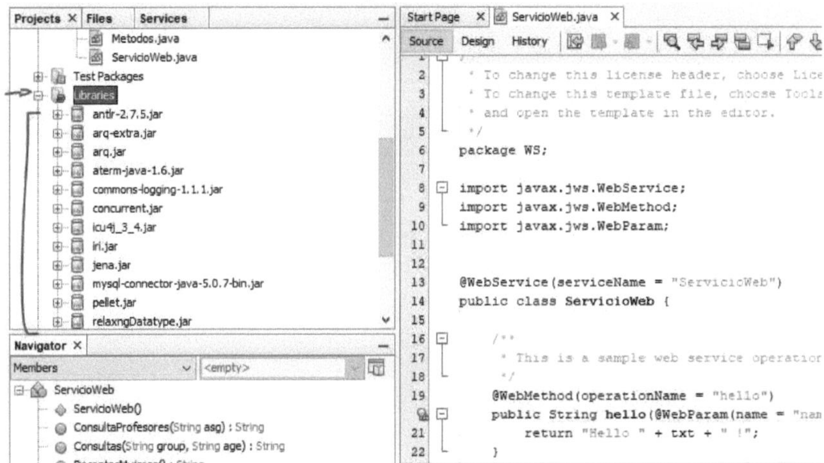

11. Now we go back to our "Methods" class that we created inside the WS package a moment ago.

Copy and paste the following imports into the class header, as shown below.

```
import java.io.IOException;
import java.io.InputStream;
import java.util.Iterator;
import org.mindswap.pellet.jena.PelletReasonerFactory;
import com.hp.hpl.jena.query.Query;
import com.hp.hpl.jena.query.QueryExecution;
```

```
import com.hp.hpl.jena.query.QueryExecutionFactory;
import com.hp.hpl.jena.query.QueryFactory;
import com.hp.hpl.jena.query.QuerySolution;
import com.hp.hpl.jena.query.ResultSet;
import com.hp.hpl.jena.rdf.model.*;
import com.hp.hpl.jena.reasoner.Reasoner;
import com.hp.hpl.jena.reasoner.ReasonerRegistry;
import com.hp.hpl.jena.reasoner.ValidityReport;
import com.hp.hpl.jena.reasoner.rulesys.GenericRuleReasoner;
import com.hp.hpl.jena.reasoner.rulesys.Rule;
import com.hp.hpl.jena.util.FileManager;
import static WS.Methods.defaultNameSpace;
```

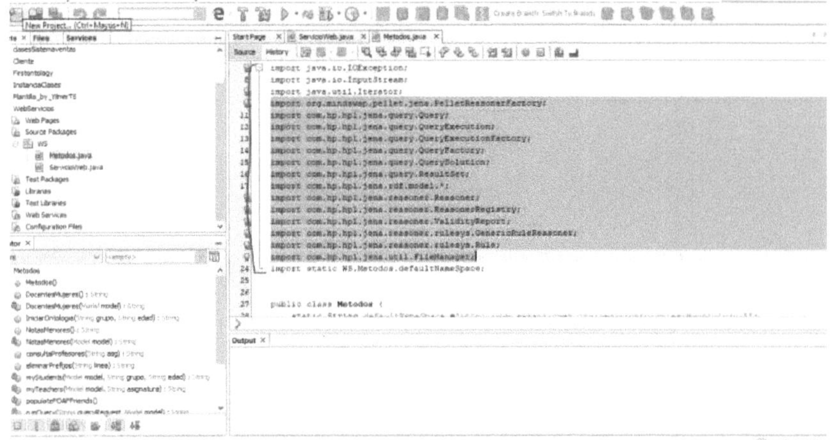

Note: If we import the libraries correctly in step 10, we will not get any error when pasting the imports in our "Methods" class.

12. Inside our public class **Methods**, we paste the following code that will access our ontology and execute the respective queries.

```
static String defaultNameSpace
="http://www.semanticweb.org/jegjo/ontologies/Myontology1#";
   Model _student = null;
   Model schema = null;
InfModel inferredStudent = null;
   String result="";
```

```java
    public String InitiateOntology(String group,String age){
 Methods myontology = new Methods();
 myontology.populateFOAFFriends();
    String res=myontology.myStudents(myontology._student,group,age);
    return res;
    }
    public String consultaProfesores(String asg){
 Methods myontology = new Methods();
 myontology.populateFOAFFriends();
    String res=myontology.myTeachers(myontology._student,asg);
    return res;
    }
    public String MinorNotes(){
 Methods myontology = new Methods();
 myontology.populateFOAFFriends();
    String res=myontology.NotesMinors(myontology._student);
    return res;
    }
    public String DocentesMujeres(){
 Methods myontology = new Methods();
 myontology.populateFOAFFriends();
    String res=myontology.DocentesMujeres(myontology._student);
    return res;
    }

    private void populateFOAFFriends(){
       _student = ModelFactory.createOntologyModel();
 InputStream inFoafInstance =
 FileManager.get().open("C:/Users/Reiner/Desktop/OntologyJava/WebServices/
 Ontologies/SampleUniversity4.owl");
       _student.read(inFoafInstance,defaultNameSpace);
       if (inFoafInstance == null) {
 result="not found";
       throw new IllegalArgumentException("File: " +
 "Ontologies/SampleUniversity4.owl" + " not found");

    }
   //inFoafInstance.close();
    }
```

```java
    private String myStudents(Model model,String group,String age){
    String res=runQuery("SELECT ? first_name ? last_name ? last_name ?age\n
"+
        "WHERE {"+
"?Student ROSCC:First_Name ? first_name.\n "+
"?Student ROSCC:is_Enrrolled ROSCC: "+group+".+".+".
"?Student ROSCC:Last_Name ? last_name.\n "+
"?Student ROSCC:Age ?age.age.age "+
        "Filter(?age >'"+age+"')}\n "+
        "Orderby ? first_name", model); //add the query string
    return res;
    }
    private String myTeachers(Model model,String asignatura){
        //listing students
        String res=runQuery("SELECT ? first_name ? last_name ? last_name
?age\n "+
        "WHERE {"+
"?Teacher ROSCC:First_Name ? first_name.\n "+
"?Teacher ROSCC:is_Imparted ROSCC: "+subject+".+".+".
"?Teacher ROSCC:Last_Name ? last_name.\n "+
"?Teacher ROSCC:Age ?age.
        "Orderby ? first_name", model); //add the query string
        return res;
    }
    private String NotasMenores(Model model){
    String res=runQuery("SELECT ? first_name ? last_name ?age ?
finish_grade\n" +
        WHERE { "WHERE" +
"Student ROSCC:First_Name ? first_name. \n" +
"?Grading ROSCC:is_A_Student ?Student.\n "+
"?Grading ROSCC:Finish_Grade ? finish_grade.grade.\n" +
" ?Student ROSCC:Last_Name ? last_name.\n" +
"?Student ROSCC:Age ?age.age.age." +
        "Filter(? finish_grade <='3')}"+
        "Orderby ? first_name", model); //add the query string
    return res;
    }
```

```java
    private String DocentesMujeres(Model model model){
      String res=runQuery("SELECT ? first_name ? last_name ? age ?
        WHERE { "WHERE" +
"?Teacher ROSCC:First_Name ? first_name. \n" +
"?Teacher ROSCC:is_Imparted ? assingment.\n "+
"?Teacher ROSCC:Last_Name ? last_name.name.\n" +
"?Teacher ROSCC:Age ?age.age.\n" +
"?Teacher ROSCC:Gender ?gender.gender.\n" +
        "Filter(?gender = 'F')}"+
        "Orderby ? first_name", model); //add the query string
      return res;
      }


    private String runQuery(String queryRequest, Model model){
StringBuffer queryStr = new StringBuffer();
    // Establish Prefixes
    //Set default Name space first
queryStr.append("PREFIX ROSCC:\n"
+"<http://www.semanticweb.org/jegjo/ontologies/Myontology1#>");
 queryStr.append("PREFIX owl: <http://www.w3.org/2002/07/owl#>) ;
 queryStr.append("PREFIX rdf" + ": <" + "http://www.w3.org/1999/02/22-rdf-
syntax-ns#" + "> ");
 queryStr.append("PREFIX rdfs" + ": <" + "http://www.w3.org/2000/01/rdf-
schema#" + "> ");
 queryStr.append("PREFIX foaf" + ": <" + "http://xmlns.com/foaf/0.1/" + ">");


    //Now add query
queryStr.append(queryRequest);
    Query query = QueryFactory.create(queryStr.toString());
QueryExecution qexec = QueryExecutionFactory.create(query, model);
    try {
ResultSet response = qexec.execSelect();
    //System.out.println("Starting search");
while( response.hasNext()){
QuerySolution soln = response.nextSolution();
RDFNode firstname = soln.get("? first_name");
RDFNode lastname = soln.get("? last_name");
RDFNode age = soln.get("?age");
if( (firstname != null) && (lastname != null) && (age != null)){
```

```java
result+="<div class="alert alert alert-info" role="alert">First Name: " +
firstname.toString() +""+" +
              " Last Name: " + lastname.toString()+
              " Age: " + age.toString()+"</div>";


    }
    else
result="No student found! ";
    }
    } finally {
qexec.close();}
    return result;
    }

    public String deletePrefixes (String line){

line=line.replace("^^http://www.semanticweb.org/jegjo/ontologies/Myontology
1#",
"");
return line;
    }
```

We would be left with something like this.

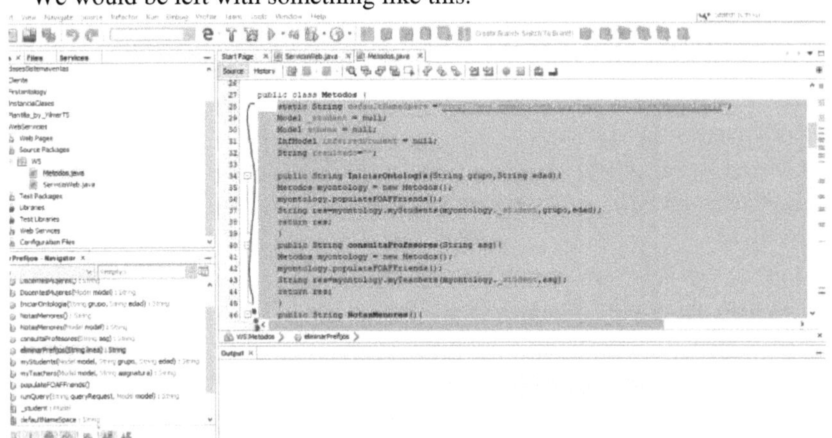

13.Now double click on the WebService file next to our methods class.

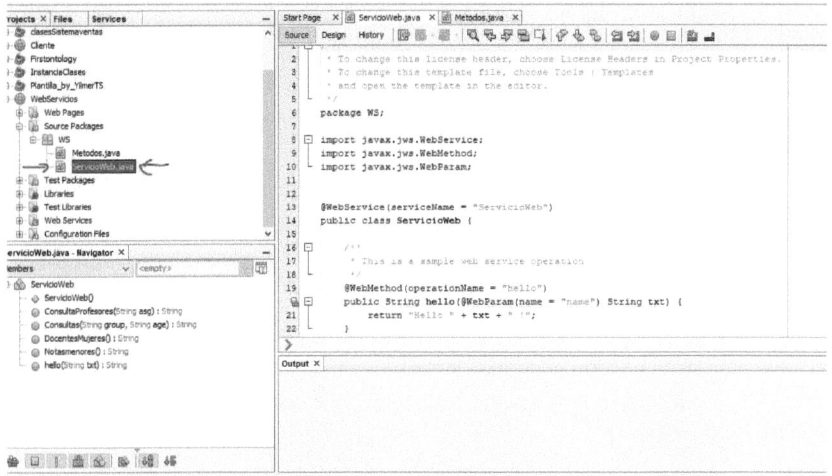

14. Then we paste the following code into it.

```java
package WS;

import javax.jws.WebService;
import javax.jws.WebMethod;
import javax.jws.WebParam;


@WebService(serviceName = "WebService")
public class WebService {

    /**
     * This is a sample web service operation
     */
    @WebMethod(operationName = "hello")
    public String hello(@WebParam(name = "name") String txt) {
        return "Hello " + txt + " !";
    }


    /**
     Web service operation
     */
    @WebMethod(operationName = "Queries")
    public String Consultas(@WebParam(name = "group") String
```

```java
group, @WebParam(name = "age") String age) {
    //TODO write your implementation code here:
Methods obj=new Methods();
    String result=obj.InitiateOntology(group,age);
    return result;
    }


    /**
     Web service operation
     */
    @WebMethod(operationName = "ConsultaProfesores")
    public String ConsultaProfesores(@WebParam(name = "asg")
String asg) {
Methods obj=new Methods();
    String result=obj.queryTeachers(asg);
    return result;
    }


    /**
     Web service operation
*/
    @WebMethod(operationName = "NotesMinors")
public String MinorNotes() {
Methods obj=new Methods();
String result=obj.MinorNotes();
    return result;
    }


    /**
     Web service operation
     */
    @WebMethod(operationName = "TeachersWomen")
    public String DocentesMujeres() {
Methods obj=new Methods();
    String result=obj.TeachersWomen();
    return result;
    }


}
```

15. Ready if we did all the same steps our web service will be created and working. To test if our WebService is working we do the following. We run our Web Service.

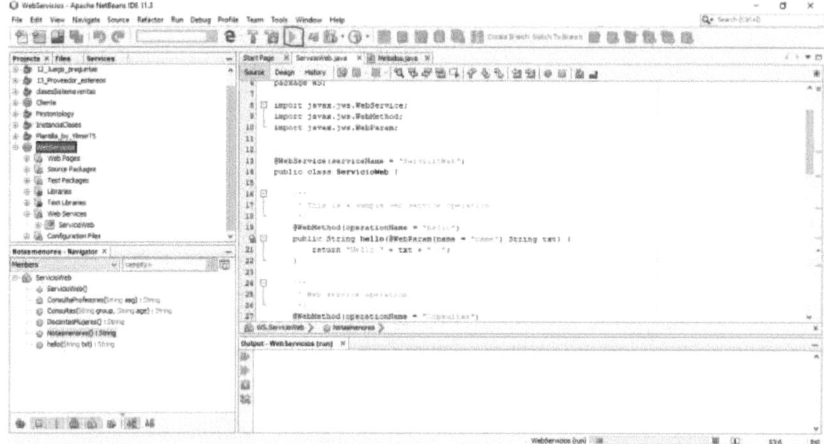

Once our web service has been executed, it will open the browser showing us that the server has been executed correctly on our system.

After that we go to netbeans and deploy the Web services folder - then right click on Web Service ->Test Web Service.

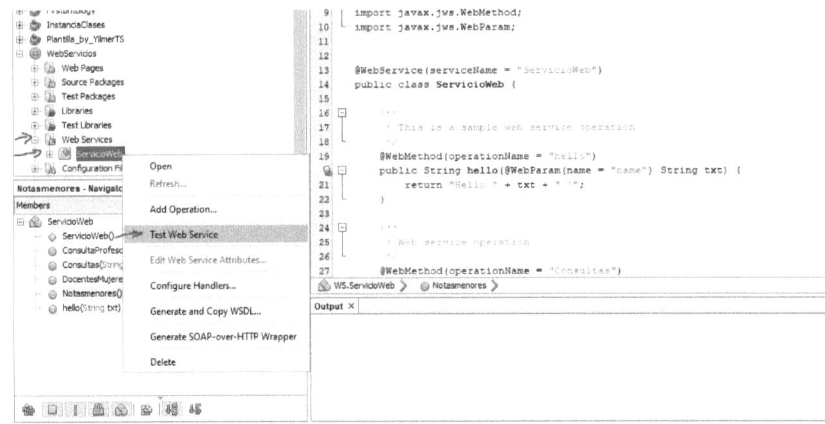

This will open the internet explorer browser and show us a default page that netbeans creates to test our web service and the queries we create.

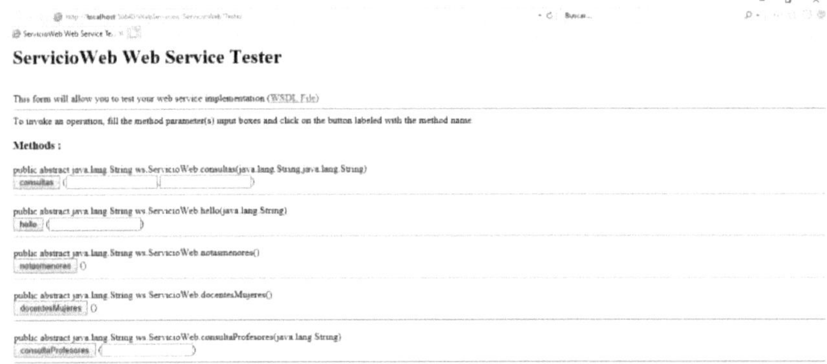

Now we just need to enter data and verify that it is querying the ontology correctly.

This form will allow you to test your web service implementation (WSDL File)

To invoke an operation, fill the method parameter(s) input boxes and click on the button labeled with the method name.

Methods :

public abstract java.lang.String ws.ServicioWeb.consultas(java.lang.String,java.lang.String)

consultas (Grp0001 , 18 ×)

public abstract java.lang.String ws.ServicioWeb.hello(java.lang.String)

We see clearly the answer to our query.

Congratulations you have created your first web service for queries in an ontology.

In the following, the use and operation of a web application that will make use of the resources of our Web Service will be shown.

A very basic java web application was created with the only purpose of consuming the web service created previously, for this purpose the web application was created with a servlet to handle all the requests and parameters sent by the user and make the connection with the web service, this servlet is also in charge of storing the answer returned by the web service and paint a page with the answer of the query.

This web application also has an index.jsp (JSP=Java Server Page) which will show us the home page when running our web application, and will also allow us to make requests to our servlet.

This would be our result.

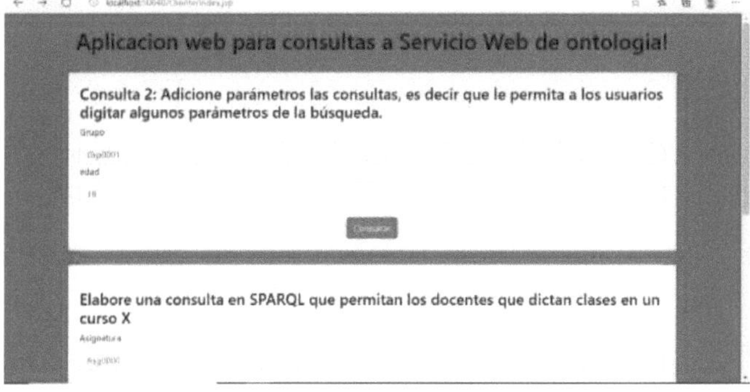

Used bookshop:

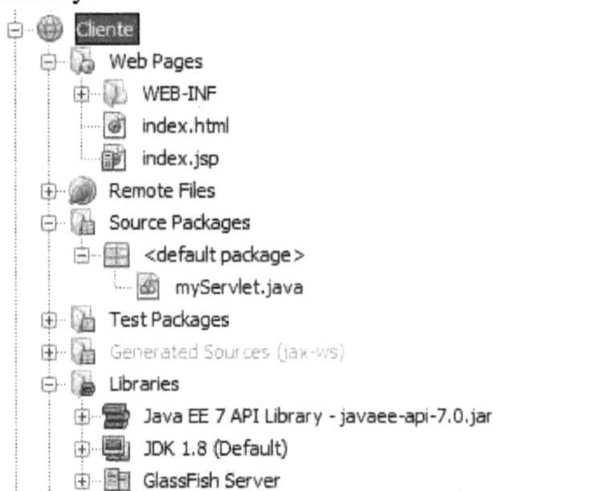

Class and file hierarchy:

References

Chen, H., Finin, T., Joshi, A (2003), An Ontology for Context Aware Pervasive Computing Environments. The Knowledge Engineering Review, vol. 18, no. 03, pp. 197 a 207

Chen, H., Perich, F., Finin, T. , Joshi, A, (2004), SOUPA: Standard Ontology for Ubiquitous and Pervasive Applications. In Mobile and Ubiquitous Systems: Networking and Services, MOBIQUITOUS 2004, pp. 258 a 276. IEEE

Wang, X.H., Zhang, D.Q., Gu, T., Pung, H.K, (2004), Ontology Based Context Modeling and Reasoning using OWL. In Pervasive Computing and Communications Workshops, 2004, pp. 18a 22. IEEE

Strang, T., Linnhoff-Popien, C., Frank, K.: CoOL, (2003), A Context Ontology Language to enable Contextual Interoperability. In 4th Int. Conf. on Distributed Applications and Interoperable Systems, pp. 236 a 247. Springer, Berlin Heidelberg

Klyne, G., Reynolds, F., Woodrow, C., Ohto, H., Hjelm, J., Butler, M.H., Tran, L, (2004), Composite Capability/Preference Profiles (CC/PP): Structure and Vocabularies 1.0. W3C Recommendation. http://www.w3.org/TR/CCPP-struct-vocab/Gu,

T., Wang, X.H., Pung, H.K., Zhang, D.Q.: (2004),. An ontology-based context model in intelligent environments. In Proceedings of communication networks and distributed systems modeling and simulation conference, pp. 270 a 275 (2004).

Xu, N., Zhang, W.S., Yang, H.D., Zhang, X.G., Xing, X, (2013), CACOnt: a ontology-based model for context modeling and reasoning. In Applied Mechanics and Materials, Vol. 347, pp. 2304 a 2310

Van Heijst, G., Schreiber, A. T., & Wielinga, B. J. (1997). Using explicit ontologies in KBS development. *International journal of human-computer studies*, *46*(2-3), 183-292.

Mizoguchi, R., Vanwelkenhuysen, J., & Ikeda, M. (1995). Task ontology for reuse of problem solving knowledge. *Towards Very Large Knowledge Bases: Knowledge Building & Knowledge Sharing, 46, 59.*

Xiang, Z., Courtot, M., Brinkman, R. R., Ruttenberg, A., & He, Y. (2010). OntoFox: web-based support for ontology reuse. *BMC research notes*, *3*(1), 175.

Jimeno-Yepes, A., Jiménez-Ruiz, E., Berlanga-Llavori, R., & Rebholz-Schuhmann, D. (2009). Reuse of terminological resources for efficient ontological engineering in Life Sciences. *BMC bioinformatics*, *10*(10), S4.

Uschold, M., & King, M. (1995). Towards a methodology for building ontologies (pp. 15-30). Edinburgh: Artificial Intelligence Applications Institute, University of Edinburgh.

Fernández-López, M. (1999). Overview of methodologies for building ontologies.

J. F. Allen. Towards a General Theory of Actions and Time. Artificial Intelligence 23:123-154, 1984.

Zhou, Q., & Fikes, R. (2002). A reusable time ontology. In *Proceeding of the AAAI Workshop on Ontologies for the Semantic Web*.

García, A. M. F., Alonso, S. S., & Sicilia, M. A. (2006). An ontology in OWL for the semantic representation of learning objects. In *V Pluridisciplinary Symposium on Design and Evaluation of Reusable Educational Content (SPDECE 2008)*.

SparQL https://www.w3.org/TR/rdf-sparql-query/

SWRL https://www.w3.org/Submission/SWRL/#4

Execution of queries in SWRL https://protege.stanford.edu/conference/2007/slides/08.01_OConnor.pdf

I want morebooks!

Buy your books fast and straightforward online - at one of world's fastest growing online book stores! Environmentally sound due to Print-on-Demand technologies.

Buy your books online at
www.morebooks.shop

Kaufen Sie Ihre Bücher schnell und unkompliziert online – auf einer der am schnellsten wachsenden Buchhandelsplattformen weltweit! Dank Print-On-Demand umwelt- und ressourcenschonend produziert.

Bücher schneller online kaufen
www.morebooks.shop

KS OmniScriptum Publishing
Brivibas gatve 197
LV-1039 Riga, Latvia
Telefax: +371 686 204 55

info@omniscriptum.com
www.omniscriptum.com

Printed by Books on Demand GmbH, Norderstedt / Germany